Hamlet

By

William Shakespeare

Hamlet

Believed to have been written between 1599 and 1601

This Edition © 2010 Simon & Brown

www.simonandbrown.com

HAMLET, PRINCE OF DENMARK

By

William Shakespeare

PERSONS REPRESENTED

Claudius, King of Denmark. ← Hamlet's fathe

Hamlet, Son to the former, and Nephew to the present King.

Polonius, Lord Chamberlain.

Horatio, Friend to Hamlet. ← Ham

Laertes, Son to Polonius.

Voltimand, Courtier.

Cornelius, Courtier.

Rosencrantz, Courtier.

Guildenstern, Courtier.

Osric, Courtier.

A Gentleman, Courtier.

A Priest.

Marcellus, Officer.

Bernardo, Officer.

Francisco, a Soldier

Reynaldo, Servant to Polonius.

Players.

Two Clowns, Grave-diggers.

Fortinbras, Prince of Norway.

A Captain.

English Ambassadors.

Ghost of Hamlet's Father.

Gertrude, Queen of Denmark, and Mother of Hamlet.

Ophelia, Daughter to Polonius.

Lords, Ladies, Officers, Soldiers, Sailors, Messengers, and other Attendants.

SCENE. Elsinore. (Platform)

ACT I.

Scene I. Elsinore. A platform before the Castle.

King Hamlet ←(Hamlet's father), died
before the play even started.

[Francisco at his post. Enter to him Bernardo.]

Ber.

Who's there?

Fran.

Nay, answer me: stand, and unfold yourself.

Ber.

Long live the king!

Fran.

Bernardo?

Ber.

He.

Fran.

You come most carefully upon your hour.

Ber.

'Tis now struck twelve. Get thee to bed, Francisco.

Fran.

For this relief much thanks: 'tis bitter cold,

And I am sick at heart.

Ber.

Have you had quiet guard?

Fran.

Not a mouse stirring.

Ber.

Well, good night.

If you do meet Horatio and Marcellus,

The rivals of my watch, bid them make haste.

Fran.

I think I hear them. – Stand, ho! Who is there?

another officer.

[Enter Horatio and Marcellus.]

Hor.

Friends to this ground.

Mar.

And liegemen to the Dane.

Fran.

Give you good-night.

Mar.

O, farewell, honest soldier;

Who hath reliev'd you?

Fran.

Bernardo has my place.

Give you good-night.

[Exit.]

Mar.

Holla! Bernardo!

Ber.

Say.

What, is Horatio there?

Hor.

A piece of him.

Ber.

Welcome, Horatio: – Welcome, good Marcellus.

Mar.

What, has this thing appear'd again to-night?

Ber.

I have seen nothing.

Mar.

Horatio says 'tis but our fantasy,

And will not let belief take hold of him

Touching this dreaded sight, twice seen of us:

Therefore I have entreated him along

With us to watch the minutes of this night;

That, if again this apparition come

He may approve our eyes and speak to it.

Hor.

Tush, tush, 'twill not appear.

Ber.

Sit down awhile,

And let us once again assail your ears,

That are so fortified against our story,

What we two nights have seen.

Hor.

Well, sit we down,

And let us hear Bernardo speak of this.

Ber.

Last night of all,

When yond same star that's westward from the pole

Had made his course to illume that part of heaven

Where now it burns, Marcellus and myself,

The bell then beating one, –

Mar.

Peace, break thee off; look where it comes again!

[Enter Ghost, armed.] ← King Hamlet (Hamlet's father)

Ber.

In the same figure, like the king that's dead.

Mar.

Thou art a scholar; speak to it, Horatio. ← Horatio is educated and he tries to talk to it.

Ber.

Looks it not like the King? mark it, Horatio.

Hor.

Most like: — it harrows me with fear and wonder.

Ber.

It would be spoke to.

Mar.

Question it, Horatio.

Hor.

What art thou, that usurp'st this time of night,

Together with that fair and warlike form

In which the majesty of buried Denmark

Did sometimes march? By heaven I charge thee, speak!

Mar.

It is offended.

Ber.

See, it stalks away!

Hor.

Stay! speak, speak! I charge thee speak!

[Exit Ghost.]

Mar.

'Tis gone, and will not answer.

Ber.

How now, Horatio! You tremble and look pale:

Is not this something more than fantasy?

What think you on't?

Hor.

Before my God, I might not this believe

Without the sensible and true avouch

Of mine own eyes.

Mar.

Is it not like the King?

Hor.

As thou art to thyself:

Such was the very armour he had on *King Fortinbras was the king of*

When he the ambitious Norway combated; *Norway. He was killed by King*

So frown'd he once when, in an angry parle, *Hamlet.*

He smote the sledded Polacks on the ice.

'Tis strange.

Mar. ← *Marcellus.*

Thus twice before, and jump at this dead hour,

With martial stalk hath he gone by our watch.

Hor. ← *Horatio.*

In what particular thought to work I know not;

But, in the gross and scope of my opinion,

This bodes some strange eruption to our state.   ← *He is more distinct in his personality. (He demands to know more.)*

Mar.

Good now, sit down, and tell me, he that knows,

Why this same strict and most observant watch

So nightly toils the subject of the land;

And why such daily cast of brazen cannon,

And foreign mart for implements of war;

Why such impress of shipwrights, whose sore task

Does not divide the Sunday from the week;

What might be toward, that this sweaty haste

Doth make the night joint-labourer with the day:

Who is't that can inform me?

Hor.

That can I;

At least, the whisper goes so. Our last king,   *King Hamlet fought king Fortinbras of Norway.*

Whose image even but now appear'd to us,

Was, as you know, by Fortinbras of Norway,

Thereto prick'd on by a most emulate pride,

Dar'd to the combat; in which our valiant Hamlet, –

For so this side of our known world esteem'd him, –

Did slay this Fortinbras; who, by a seal'd compact,

Well ratified by law and heraldry, ← *legal document*

Did forfeit, with his life, all those his lands,

Which he stood seiz'd of, to the conqueror: ← *he got the land if the person lost.*

Against the which, a moiety competent *(young Fortinbras is not happy about it.)*

Was gaged by our king; which had return'd

To the inheritance of Fortinbras,

Had he been vanquisher; as by the same cov'nant,

And carriage of the article design'd,

His fell to Hamlet. Now, sir, young Fortinbras,

Of unimproved mettle hot and full,

Hath in the skirts of Norway, here and there,

Shark'd up a list of lawless resolutes,

For food and diet, to some enterprise

That hath a stomach in't; which is no other, –

As it doth well appear unto our state, –

But to recover of us, by strong hand,

And terms compulsatory, those foresaid lands

So by his father lost: and this, I take it,

Is the main motive of our preparations,

The source of this our watch, and the chief head

Of this post-haste and romage in the land.

Ber.

I think it be no other but e'en so:

Well may it sort, that this portentous figure

Comes armed through our watch; so like the king

That was and is the question of these wars.

Hor.

A mote it is to trouble the mind's eye.

In the most high and palmy state of Rome,

A little ere the mightiest Julius fell, ←— 1st allusion to Julius Cesar.

The graves stood tenantless, and the sheeted dead

Did squeak and gibber in the Roman streets;

As, stars with trains of fire and dews of blood,

Disasters in the sun; and the moist star,

Upon whose influence Neptune's empire stands, ←— second allusion (mythical place: Atlantis)

Was sick almost to doomsday with eclipse:

And even the like precurse of fierce events, –

As harbingers preceding still the fates,

And prologue to the omen coming on, –

Have heaven and earth together demonstrated

Unto our climature and countrymen. –

But, soft, behold! lo, where it comes again!

[Re-enter Ghost.]

I'll cross it, though it blast me. – Stay, illusion!

If thou hast any sound, or use of voice,

Speak to me:

If there be any good thing to be done,

That may to thee do ease, and, race to me,

Speak to me:

If thou art privy to thy country's fate,

Which, happily, foreknowing may avoid,

O, speak!

Or if thou hast uphoarded in thy life

Extorted treasure in the womb of earth,

For which, they say, you spirits oft walk in death,

[The cock crows.]

Speak of it: – stay, and speak! – Stop it, Marcellus!

Mar.

Shall I strike at it with my partisan?

Hor.

Do, if it will not stand.

Ber.

'Tis here!

Hor.

'Tis here!

Mar.

'Tis gone!

[Exit Ghost.]

We do it wrong, being so majestical,

To offer it the show of violence;

For it is, as the air, invulnerable,

And our vain blows malicious mockery.

Ber.

It was about to speak, when the cock crew.

Hor.

And then it started, like a guilty thing

Upon a fearful summons. I have heard

The cock, that is the trumpet to the morn,

Doth with his lofty and shrill-sounding throat

Awake the god of day; and at his warning,

Whether in sea or fire, in earth or air,

The extravagant and erring spirit hies

To his confine: and of the truth herein

This present object made probation.

Mar.

It faded on the crowing of the cock.

Some say that ever 'gainst that season comes

Wherein our Saviour's birth is celebrated, ← 3rd allusion
Jesus's birth.
The bird of dawning singeth all night long;

And then, they say, no spirit dare stir abroad;

The nights are wholesome; then no planets strike,

No fairy takes, nor witch hath power to charm;

So hallow'd and so gracious is the time.

Hor.

So have I heard, and do in part believe it.

But, look, the morn, in russet mantle clad,

Walks o'er the dew of yon high eastward hill:

Break we our watch up: and by my advice,

Let us impart what we have seen to-night

Unto young Hamlet; for, upon my life,

This spirit, dumb to us, will speak to him:

Do you consent we shall acquaint him with it,

As needful in our loves, fitting our duty?

Mar.

Let's do't, I pray; and I this morning know

Where we shall find him most conveniently.

[Exeunt.]

Scene II. Elsinore. A room of state in the Castle.

[Enter the King, Queen, Hamlet, Polonius, Laertes, Voltimand,

Cornelius, Lords, and Attendant.]

King.

Though yet of Hamlet our dear brother's death 1st group

The memory be green, and that it us befitted · The king talks a lot

To bear our hearts in grief, and our whole kingdom (picture

someone who's
To be contracted in one brow of woe; just crowned
and his
Yet so far hath discretion fought with nature brother died.
claudius gets
That we with wisest sorrow think on him, married to
Gertrude.)
Together with remembrance of ourselves.

Therefore our sometime sister, now our queen,

Th' imperial jointress to this warlike state,

Have we, as 'twere with a defeated joy, –

With an auspicious and one dropping eye,

With mirth in funeral, and with dirge in marriage,

In equal scale weighing delight and dole, –

Taken to wife; nor have we herein barr'd

Your better wisdoms, which have freely gone

With this affair along: – or all, our thanks.

Now follows, that you know, young Fortinbras,

Holding a weak supposal of our worth,

Or thinking by our late dear brother's death

Our state to be disjoint and out of frame,

Colleagued with this dream of his advantage,

He hath not fail'd to pester us with message,

Importing the surrender of those lands

Lost by his father, with all bonds of law,

To our most valiant brother. So much for him, –

Now for ourself and for this time of meeting:

Thus much the business is: – we have here writ

To Norway, uncle of young Fortinbras, –

Who, impotent and bed-rid, scarcely hears

Of this his nephew's purpose, – to suppress

His further gait herein; in that the levies,

The lists, and full proportions are all made

Out of his subject: – and we here dispatch

You, good Cornelius, and you, Voltimand,

For bearers of this greeting to old Norway;

Giving to you no further personal power

To business with the king, more than the scope

Of these dilated articles allow.

Farewell; and let your haste commend your duty.

Cor. and Volt.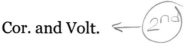

In that and all things will we show our duty.

King.

We doubt it nothing: heartily farewell.

[Exeunt Voltimand and Cornelius.]

And now, Laertes, what's the news with you?

You told us of some suit; what is't, Laertes?

You cannot speak of reason to the Dane,

And lose your voice: what wouldst thou beg, Laertes,

That shall not be my offer, not thy asking?

The head is not more native to the heart,

The hand more instrumental to the mouth,

Than is the throne of Denmark to thy father.

What wouldst thou have, Laertes?

Laer.  ← 3rd

Dread my lord,

Your leave and favour to return to France;

From whence though willingly I came to Denmark,

To show my duty in your coronation;

Yet now, I must confess, that duty done,

My thoughts and wishes bend again toward France,

And bow them to your gracious leave and pardon.

King.

Have you your father's leave? What says Polonius?

Pol.  ← 4th

He hath, my lord, wrung from me my slow leave

By laboursome petition; and at last

Upon his will I seal'd my hard consent:

I do beseech you, give him leave to go.

King.

Take thy fair hour, Laertes; time be thine,

And thy best graces spend it at thy will! –

But now, my cousin Hamlet, and my son –

Polonius does not want Laertes to leave.

Ham.

[Aside.] A little more than kin, and less than kind!

King.

How is it that the clouds still hang on you? ← *1st pun*

Ham.

Not so, my lord; I am too much i' the sun. ← *2nd pun*

Queen.

Good Hamlet, cast thy nighted colour off,

And let thine eye look like a friend on Denmark.

Do not for ever with thy vailed lids

Seek for thy noble father in the dust:

Thou know'st 'tis common, – all that lives must die,

Passing through nature to eternity. ←

Hamlet is not happy and has too much black bile. He does not care whether anyone likes it or not.

She wants him to be a prince.

Ham.

Ay, madam, it is common.

Queen.

If it be,

Why seems it so particular with thee?

Ham. ⟵ *Hamlet is greiving over his father's death.*

Seems, madam! Nay, it is; I know not seems.

'Tis not alone my inky cloak, good mother,

Nor customary suits of solemn black,

Nor windy suspiration of forc'd breath,

No, nor the fruitful river in the eye,

Hamlet is saying that he is not "disguised" like this, he is like this. ⟵(greiving over his father.)

Nor the dejected 'havior of the visage,

Together with all forms, moods, shows of grief,

That can denote me truly: these, indeed, seem;

For they are actions that a man might play;

But I have that within which passeth show;

These but the trappings and the suits of woe.

King. ← *Claudius*

'Tis sweet and commendable in your nature, Hamlet,

To give these mourning duties to your father;

But, you must know, your father lost a father;

That father lost, lost his; and the survivor bound,

Claudius shows his empathy for Hamlet.

In filial obligation, for some term

To do obsequious sorrow: but to persevere

In obstinate condolement is a course

Of impious stubbornness; 'tis unmanly grief;

It shows a will most incorrect to heaven;

A heart unfortified, a mind impatient;

An understanding simple and unschool'd;

Claudius is insulting Hamlet.

For what we know must be, and is as common

As any the most vulgar thing to sense,

Why should we, in our peevish opposition,

Take it to heart? Fie! 'tis a fault to heaven,

A fault against the dead, a fault to nature,

irregular + acting wrongful.

To reason most absurd; whose common theme

Is death of fathers, and who still hath cried,

From the first corse till he that died to-day,

'This must be so.' We pray you, throw to earth

This unprevailing woe; and think of us

As of a father: for let the world take note

He reminds Hamlet that he is future king.

You are the most immediate to our throne;

And with no less nobility of love

Than that which dearest father bears his son

Do I impart toward you. For your intent

In going back to school in Wittenberg, ←— *Laertes is going back to France.*

It is most retrograde to our desire:

And we beseech you bend you to remain ←— *Claudius is asking / requesting Hamlet to stay.*

Here in the cheer and comfort of our eye,

Our chiefest courtier, cousin, and our son.

Queen.

Let not thy mother lose her prayers, Hamlet:

I pray thee stay with us; go not to Wittenberg.

Ham.

I shall in all my best obey you, madam. →*blatant ignoring answers his mom instead of claudius.*

King.

Why, 'tis a loving and a fair reply:

Be as ourself in Denmark. – Madam, come;

This gentle and unforc'd accord of Hamlet

Sits smiling to my heart: in grace whereof,

No jocund health that Denmark drinks to-day

But the great cannon to the clouds shall tell;

And the king's rouse the heaven shall bruit again,

Re-speaking earthly thunder. Come away.

Claudius ignores Hamlet

[Exeunt all but Hamlet.]

Ham. ← *This is Hamlet's (first sililoqouy.)*

O that this too too solid flesh would melt,

Thaw, and resolve itself into a dew!

Or that the Everlasting had not fix'd

His canon 'gainst self-slaughter! O God! O God!

Hamlet is having suicidal thoughts (sad, anger, melancholy, bitter, argumentative)

How weary, stale, flat, and unprofitable

Seem to me all the uses of this world!

Fie on't! O fie! 'tis an unweeded garden,

That grows to seed; things rank and gross in nature

disgusted

Possess it merely. That it should come to this!

But two months dead! – nay, not so much, not two:

So excellent a king; that was, to this,

Hyperion to a satyr; so loving to my mother,

[handwritten: sun   goat → claudius]

That he might not beteem the winds of heaven

[handwritten: Gertrude]

Visit her face too roughly. Heaven and earth!

Must I remember? Why, she would hang on him

As if increase of appetite had grown

By what it fed on: and yet, within a month, –

[handwritten annotation: How Gertrude acted when Hamlet's real father was alive.]

Let me not think on't, – Frailty, thy name is woman!

[handwritten: ← Gertrude?]

A little month; or ere those shoes were old

With which she followed my poor father's body

Like Niobe, all tears; – why she, even she, –

[handwritten: this is related to Greek mythology]

O God! a beast that wants discourse of reason,

Would have mourn'd longer, – married with mine uncle,

My father's brother; but no more like my father

Than I to Hercules: within a month;

[handwritten annotation: Hamlet has hurt + bitter feelings towards claudius.]

Ere yet the salt of most unrighteous tears

Had left the flushing in her galled eyes,

She married: – O, most wicked speed, to post

With such dexterity to incestuous sheets!

It is not, nor it cannot come to good;

But break my heart, – for I must hold my tongue!

[Enter Horatio, Marcellus, and Bernardo.]

Hor.

Hail to your lordship!

Ham.

I am glad to see you well:

Horatio, – or I do forget myself.

Hor.

The same, my lord, and your poor servant ever.

Ham.

Sir, my good friend; I'll change that name with you:

And what make you from Wittenberg, Horatio? –

Marcellus?

Mar.

My good lord, –

Ham.

I am very glad to see you. – Good even, sir. –

But what, in faith, make you from Wittenberg?

Hor.

A truant disposition, good my lord.

Ham.

I would not hear your enemy say so;

Nor shall you do my ear that violence,

To make it truster of your own report

Against yourself: I know you are no truant.

But what is your affair in Elsinore?

We'll teach you to drink deep ere you depart.

Hamlet suspects that Claudius killed his father king Hamlet.

Hor.

My lord, I came to see your father's funeral.

Ham.

I prithee do not mock me, fellow-student.

I think it was to see my mother's wedding.

Hor.

Indeed, my lord, it follow'd hard upon.

Ham.

Thrift, thrift, Horatio! The funeral bak'd meats

Did coldly furnish forth the marriage tables.

Would I had met my dearest foe in heaven

Or ever I had seen that day, Horatio! –

My father, – methinks I see my father.

Hamlet sees his father.

The ghost has appeared?

Hor.

Where, my lord?

Ham.

In my mind's eye, Horatio.

Hor.

I saw him once; he was a goodly king.

Ham.

He was a man, take him for all in all,

I shall not look upon his like again.

Hor.

My lord, I think I saw him yesternight.

(the night before)...
last—night

Horatio thinks that he saw his father the night before.

Ham.

Saw who?

Hor.

My lord, the king your father.

Ham.

The King my father!

Hor.

Season your admiration for awhile

With an attent ear, till I may deliver,

Upon the witness of these gentlemen,

This marvel to you.

Ham.

For God's love let me hear.

Hor.

Two nights together had these gentlemen,

Marcellus and Bernardo, on their watch

In the dead vast and middle of the night,

Been thus encounter'd. A figure like your father,

Armed at point exactly, cap-a-pe,

Appears before them and with solemn march

Goes slow and stately by them: thrice he walk'd

By their oppress'd and fear-surprised eyes,

Within his truncheon's length; whilst they, distill'd

Almost to jelly with the act of fear,

Stand dumb, and speak not to him. This to me

In dreadful secrecy impart they did;

And I with them the third night kept the watch:

Where, as they had deliver'd, both in time,

Form of the thing, each word made true and good,

The apparition comes: I knew your father;

These hands are not more like.

Ham.

But where was this?

Mar.

My lord, upon the platform where we watch'd.

Ham.

Did you not speak to it?

Hor.

My lord, I did;

But answer made it none: yet once methought

It lifted up it head, and did address

Itself to motion, like as it would speak:

But even then the morning cock crew loud,

And at the sound it shrunk in haste away,

And vanish'd from our sight.

Ham.

'Tis very strange.

Hor.

As I do live, my honour'd lord, 'tis true;

And we did think it writ down in our duty

To let you know of it.

Ham.

Indeed, indeed, sirs, but this troubles me.

Hold you the watch to-night?

Mar. and Ber.

We do, my lord.

Ham.

Arm'd, say you?

Both.

Arm'd, my lord.

Ham.

From top to toe?

Both.

My lord, from head to foot.

Ham.

Then saw you not his face?

Hor.

O, yes, my lord: he wore his beaver up.

Ham.

What, look'd he frowningly?

Hor.

A countenance more in sorrow than in anger.

Ham.

Pale or red?

Hor.

Nay, very pale.

Ham.

And fix'd his eyes upon you?

Hor.

Most constantly.

Ham.

I would I had been there.

Hor.

It would have much amaz'd you.

Ham.

Very like, very like. Stay'd it long?

Hor.

While one with moderate haste might tell a hundred.

Mar. and Ber.

Longer, longer.

Hor.

Not when I saw't.

Ham.

His beard was grizzled, – no?

Hor.

It was, as I have seen it in his life,

A sable silver'd.

Ham.

I will watch to-night;

Perchance 'twill walk again.

Hor.

I warr'nt it will.

Hamlet is planning to go on watch with Horatio, Marcellus, and Bernardo, to see if his father comes.

Ham.

If it assume my noble father's person,

I'll speak to it, though hell itself should gape

And bid me hold my peace. I pray you all,

If you have hitherto conceal'd this sight,

Let it be tenable in your silence still;

And whatsoever else shall hap to-night,

Give it an understanding, but no tongue:

I will requite your loves. So, fare ye well:

Upon the platform, 'twixt eleven and twelve,

I'll visit you.

All.

Our duty to your honour.

Ham.

Your loves, as mine to you: farewell.

[Exeunt Horatio, Marcellus, and Bernardo.]

He basically goes on the night watch with his father.

☆ FORESHADOWING #1

My father's spirit in arms! All is not well;

I doubt some foul play: would the night were come!

Till then sit still, my soul: foul deeds will rise,

Though all the earth o'erwhelm them, to men's eyes.

Hamlet took the spot of Bernardo and Marcellus to go on watch with them.

He makes a comment at the end.

[Exit.]

father ↓

Scene III. A room in Polonius's house.

[Enter Laertes and Ophelia.] ← *Hamlet's girlfriend*

brother   daughter

Laer.

My necessaries are embark'd: farewell:

And, sister, as the winds give benefit

And convoy is assistant, do not sleep,

But let me hear from you. ←

Laertes is going to France.

Laertes wants Ophelia to write to him.

Oph.

Do you doubt that?

Laer.

For Hamlet, and the trifling of his favour,

Hold it a fashion, and a toy in blood:

A violet in the youth of primy nature,

Forward, not permanent, sweet, not lasting;

The perfume and suppliance of a minute;

No more.

He tells her to stay away from Hamlet.

Oph.

No more but so?

Laer.

Think it no more:

For nature, crescent, does not grow alone

In thews and bulk; but as this temple waxes,

The inward service of the mind and soul

Grows wide withal. Perhaps he loves you now;

And now no soil nor cautel doth besmirch

He might love her now, but it will not last for a long time.

The virtue of his will: but you must fear,

His greatness weigh'd, his will is not his own;

For he himself is subject to his birth:

Laertes says that Hamlet is a prince and he is subject to his birth.

He may not, as unvalu'd persons do,

Carve for himself; for on his choice depends

The safety and health of this whole state;

And therefore must his choice be circumscrib'd

Unto the voice and yielding of that body

Whereof he is the head. Then if he says he loves you,

It fits your wisdom so far to believe it

As he in his particular act and place

May give his saying deed; which is no further

Than the main voice of Denmark goes withal.

Then weigh what loss your honour may sustain

If with too credent ear you list his songs,

Or lose your heart, or your chaste treasure open

He might sleep w/ her, but — her virginity.

To his unmaster'd importunity.

Fear it, Ophelia, fear it, my dear sister;

And keep you in the rear of your affection,

Out of the shot and danger of desire.

The chariest maid is prodigal enough

most cautious *prude*

← Even the good girls get bad reputations.

If she unmask her beauty to the moon:

He tells her why to stay away from Hamlet.

Virtue itself scopes not calumnious strokes:

The canker galls the infants of the spring

Too oft before their buttons be disclos'd:

And in the morn and liquid dew of youth

Contagious blastments are most imminent.

Be wary then; best safety lies in fear: ← *Be careful and weary!*

Youth to itself rebels, though none else near.

Oph.

I shall th' effect of this good lesson keep

As watchman to my heart. But, good my brother,

she tells him that she'll take care of himself.

Do not, as some ungracious pastors do,

she compares him to...

Show me the steep and thorny way to heaven;

Whilst, like a puff'd and reckless libertine,

Himself the primrose path of dalliance treads

And recks not his own read.

Laer.

O, fear me not. ← *do not worry for me.*

I stay too long: – but here my father comes.

[Enter Polonius.] ← *Ophelia's father*

A double blessing is a double grace; *He gives*
Occasion smiles upon a second leave. — *Laertes advice.*

Pol.

Yet here, Laertes! aboard, aboard, for shame! *Laertes*
is about
The wind sits in the shoulder of your sail, *to go*
for France.
And you are stay'd for. There, – my blessing with thee!

[Laying his hand on Laertes's head.]

And these few precepts in thy memory

Look thou character. Give thy thoughts no tongue,

Nor any unproportion'd thought his act.

Be thou familiar, but by no means vulgar.

Those friends thou hast, and their adoption tried,

Grapple them unto thy soul with hoops of steel;

But do not dull thy palm with entertainment

Of each new-hatch'd, unfledg'd comrade. Beware

Of entrance to a quarrel; but, being in,

Bear't that the opposed may beware of thee.

[handwritten: Polonius tells Laertes to be careful.]

Give every man thine ear, but few thy voice:

Take each man's censure, but reserve thy judgment.

Costly thy habit as thy purse can buy,

But not express'd in fancy; rich, not gaudy:

For the apparel oft proclaims the man;

And they in France of the best rank and station

Are most select and generous chief in that.

Neither a borrower nor a lender be:

For loan oft loses both itself and friend;

And borrowing dulls the edge of husbandry.

This above all, – to thine own self be true;

[handwritten: Polonius says this to Laertes, and tells him to be careful.]

And it must follow, as the night the day,

Thou canst not then be false to any man.

Farewell: my blessing season this in thee!

Laer.

Most humbly do I take my leave, my lord.

Pol.

The time invites you; go, your servants tend.

Laer.

Farewell, Ophelia; and remember well

What I have said to you.

Oph.

'Tis in my memory lock'd,

And you yourself shall keep the key of it.

Laer.

Farewell.

[Exit.]

Pol.

What is't, Ophelia, he hath said to you?

Oph.

So please you, something touching the Lord Hamlet.

Pol.

Marry, well bethought:

'Tis told me he hath very oft of late

Given private time to you; and you yourself

Have of your audience been most free and bounteous;

If it be so, – as so 'tis put on me,

And that in way of caution, – I must tell you

You do not understand yourself so clearly

As it behooves my daughter and your honour.

What is between you? give me up the truth.

Oph.

He hath, my lord, of late made many tenders

Of his affection to me.

Pol.

Affection! pooh! you speak like a green girl,

Unsifted in such perilous circumstance.

Do you believe his tenders, as you call them?

Polonius is convincing Ophelia

Oph.

I do not know, my lord, what I should think.

Pol.

Marry, I'll teach you: think yourself a baby;

That you have ta'en these tenders for true pay,

Which are not sterling. Tender yourself more dearly;

Or, – not to crack the wind of the poor phrase,

Wronging it thus, – you'll tender me a fool.

Oph.

My lord, he hath importun'd me with love

In honourable fashion.

Pol.

Ay, fashion you may call it; go to, go to.

Oph.

And hath given countenance to his speech, my lord,

With almost all the holy vows of heaven.

Pol.

Ay, springes to catch woodcocks. I do know,

When the blood burns, how prodigal the soul

Lends the tongue vows: these blazes, daughter,

Giving more light than heat, – extinct in both,

Even in their promise, as it is a-making, –

You must not take for fire. From this time

Be something scanter of your maiden presence;

Set your entreatments at a higher rate

Than a command to parley. For Lord Hamlet,

Believe so much in him, that he is young;

And with a larger tether may he walk

Than may be given you: in few, Ophelia,

Do not believe his vows; for they are brokers, –

Not of that dye which their investments show,

But mere implorators of unholy suits,

Breathing like sanctified and pious bawds,

The better to beguile. This is for all, –

I would not, in plain terms, from this time forth

Have you so slander any moment leisure

As to give words or talk with the Lord Hamlet.

Look to't, I charge you; come your ways.

Oph.

I shall obey, my lord.

[Exeunt.]

Scene IV. The platform. *(Hamlet's joining the boys ~~to~~ ~~see~~ ~~go~~ on a night watch for king Hamlet's ghost.*

[Enter Hamlet, Horatio, and Marcellus.]

Ham.

The air bites shrewdly; it is very cold. ←—— *It is night-time (the boys are on the platform on the lookout for king Hamlet.)*

Hor.

It is a nipping and an eager air.

Ham.

What hour now?

Hor.

I think it lacks of twelve.

Mar.

No, it is struck.

Hor.

Indeed? I heard it not: then draws near the season

Wherein the spirit held his wont to walk.

[A flourish of trumpets, and ordnance shot off within.]

What does this mean, my lord?

Ham.

The King doth wake to-night and takes his rouse,

Keeps wassail, and the swaggering up-spring reels;

And, as he drains his draughts of Rhenish down,

they went out to party.

The kettle-drum and trumpet thus bray out

The triumph of his pledge.

Hor.

Is it a custom?

Ham.

Ay, marry, is't;

But to my mind, – though I am native here,

And to the manner born, – it is a custom

More honour'd in the breach than the observance.

This heavy-headed revel east and west

Makes us traduc'd and tax'd of other nations:

They clepe us drunkards, and with swinish phrase

Soil our addition; and, indeed, it takes

From our achievements, though perform'd at height,

The pith and marrow of our attribute.

So oft it chances in particular men

That, for some vicious mole of nature in them,

As in their birth, – wherein they are not guilty,

Since nature cannot choose his origin, –

By the o'ergrowth of some complexion,

Oft breaking down the pales and forts of reason;

[Handwritten annotations: "1st prob. He is talking about how other countries approve it." / "2nd problem. They get called pigs because they just drink" / "3rd problem"]

Or by some habit, that too much o'er-leavens

The form of plausive manners; – that these men, –

Carrying, I say, the stamp of one defect,

Being nature's livery, or fortune's star, –

Their virtues else, – be they as pure as grace,

As infinite as man may undergo, –

Shall in the general censure take corruption

From that particular fault: the dram of eale

3rd: Even the smartest people act like idiots.

Doth all the noble substance often doubt

* Hamlet does not drink

To his own scandal.

Hor.

Look, my lord, it comes!

[Enter Ghost.]

Ham.

Angels and ministers of grace defend us! –

Be thou a spirit of health or goblin damn'd,

Bring with thee airs from heaven or blasts from hell,

Hamlet Is it a good or bad ghost?

Be thy intents wicked or charitable,

Thou com'st in such a questionable shape

That I will speak to thee: I'll call thee Hamlet,

King, father, royal Dane; O, answer me!

Let me not burst in ignorance; but tell

Why thy canoniz'd bones, hearsed in death,

Have burst their cerements; why the sepulchre,

Wherein we saw thee quietly in-urn'd,

Hath op'd his ponderous and marble jaws

To cast thee up again! What may this mean,

That thou, dead corse, again in complete steel,

Revisit'st thus the glimpses of the moon,

Making night hideous, and we fools of nature

So horridly to shake our disposition

With thoughts beyond the reaches of our souls?

Say, why is this? wherefore? what should we do?

[Ghost beckons Hamlet.]

Hor.

It beckons you to go away with it,

As if it some impartment did desire

To you alone.

Mar.

Look with what courteous action

It waves you to a more removed ground:

But do not go with it!

Hor.

No, by no means.

Ham.

It will not speak; then will I follow it.

Hor.

Do not, my lord.

Ham.

Why, what should be the fear?

I do not set my life at a pin's fee;

And for my soul, what can it do to that,

Being a thing immortal as itself?

It waves me forth again; — I'll follow it.

Hor.

What if it tempt you toward the flood, my lord,

Or to the dreadful summit of the cliff

That beetles o'er his base into the sea,

And there assume some other horrible form

Which might deprive your sovereignty of reason,

And draw you into madness? think of it:

The very place puts toys of desperation,

Without more motive, into every brain

That looks so many fadoms to the sea

And hears it roar beneath.

Ham.

It waves me still. —

Go on; I'll follow thee.

Mar.

You shall not go, my lord.

Ham.

Hold off your hands.

Hor.

Be rul'd; you shall not go.

Ham.

My fate cries out,

And makes each petty artery in this body

As hardy as the Nemean lion's nerve. –

[Ghost beckons.]

Still am I call'd; – unhand me, gentlemen; –

[Breaking free from them.]

By heaven, I'll make a ghost of him that lets me! –

I say, away! – Go on; I'll follow thee.

[Exeunt Ghost and Hamlet.]

Hor.

He waxes desperate with imagination.

Mar.

Let's follow; 'tis not fit thus to obey him.

Horatio and Marcellus are worried that if the ghost is bad, then he will drag him with him (the ghost)

Hor.

Have after. – To what issue will this come?

Mar.

Something is rotten in the state of Denmark.

Hor.

Heaven will direct it.

Mar.

Nay, let's follow him.

[Exeunt.]

Scene V. A more remote part of the Castle.

[Enter Ghost and Hamlet.]

Ham.

Whither wilt thou lead me? speak! I'll go no further.

Ghost.

Mark me.

Ham.

I will.

Ghost.

My hour is almost come,

When I to sulph'uous and tormenting flames

Must render up myself.

King Hamlet is in purgatory.

Ham.

Alas, poor ghost!

Ghost.

Pity me not, but lend thy serious hearing

To what I shall unfold.

Ham.

Speak; I am bound to hear.

Ghost.

So art thou to revenge, when thou shalt hear. ⟵ revenge

Ham.

What?

Ghost.

I am thy father's spirit; ⟵ He tells Hamlet that he needs to take revenge on claudius.

Doom'd for a certain term to walk the night,

And for the day confin'd to wastein fires,

Till the foul crimes done in my days of nature

Are burnt and purg'd away. But that I am forbid

To tell the secrets of my prison-house,

I could a tale unfold whose lightest word

Would harrow up thy soul; freeze thy young blood;

Make thy two eyes, like stars, start from their spheres;

Thy knotted and combined locks to part,

And each particular hair to stand on end

Like quills upon the fretful porcupine:

But this eternal blazon must not be

To ears of flesh and blood. – List, list, O, list! –

If thou didst ever thy dear father love –

Ham.

O God!

Ghost.

Revenge his foul and most unnatural murder. ← Take revenge on claudius

Ham.

Murder! ← King Hamlet's murder

Ghost.

Murder most foul, as in the best it is;

But this most foul, strange, and unnatural.

Ham.

Haste me to know't, that I, with wings as swift

As meditation or the thoughts of love,

May sweep to my revenge.

Ghost.

I find thee apt;

And duller shouldst thou be than the fat weed

That rots itself in ease on Lethe wharf,

Wouldst thou not stir in this. Now, Hamlet, hear.

'Tis given out that, sleeping in my orchard,

snake ← Claudius

A serpent stung me; so the whole ear of Denmark

Is by a forged process of my death

Rankly abus'd; but know, thou noble youth,

The serpent that did sting thy father's life

Now wears his crown. ← Claudius

4th pun
king Hamlet tells Hamlet to take revenge on claudius, and tells him how he died. He mentions Gertrude.

Ham.

O my prophetic soul!

Mine uncle! ← Claudius

Ghost.

Ay, that incestuous, that adulterate beast, ← Claudius won Gertrude's heart.

With witchcraft of his wit, with traitorous gifts, –

O wicked wit and gifts, that have the power

So to seduce! – won to his shameful lust

The will of my most seeming-virtuous queen: He mentions Gertrude.

O Hamlet, what a falling-off was there! → of their love. mentions how

From me, whose love was of that dignity they were

That it went hand in hand even with the vow

I made to her in marriage; and to decline → lust

Upon a wretch whose natural gifts were poor

To those of mine!

But virtue, as it never will be mov'd, He explains how different Gertrude is now.

Though lewdness court it in a shape of heaven;

So lust, though to a radiant angel link'd,

Will sate itself in a celestial bed

And prey on garbage.

But soft! methinks I scent the morning air;

Hamlet

Brief let me be. – Sleeping within my orchard,

My custom always of the afternoon, *routine*

Upon my secure hour thy uncle stole, *sneaky way*

With juice of cursed (hebenon) in a vial, *poison*

And in the porches of my ears did pour *5th pun.*

The (leperous) distilment; whose effect *leprousy.*

Holds such an enmity with blood of man

That, swift as quicksilver, it courses through

The natural gates and alleys of the body;

And with a sudden vigour it doth posset

And curd, like eager droppings into milk,

The thin and wholesome blood; so did it mine;

And a most instant tetter bark'd about,

Most lazar-like, with vile and loathsome crust *the skin erupts..*

All my smooth body.

Thus was I, sleeping, by a brother's hand,

Of life, of crown, of queen, at once dispatch'd:

Cut off even in the blossoms of my sin, * *NOTE: king Hamlet did not get that.*

Unhous'led, disappointed, unanel'd;

No reckoning made, but sent to my account

With all my imperfections on my head:

King Hamlet goes on to describe how he died and what caused him to die. He wants Hamlet to take revenge on Claudius for what he has done.

If you're dying you call the priest and tell him to please get rid of his sins so he can go to Heaven.

O, horrible! O, horrible! most horrible!

If thou hast nature in thee, bear it not;

Let not the royal bed of Denmark be

A couch for luxury and damned incest.

But, howsoever thou pursu'st this act,

Taint not thy mind, nor let thy soul contrive

Against thy mother aught: leave her to heaven,

And to those thorns that in her bosom lodge,

To prick and sting her. Fare thee well at once!

The glowworm shows the matin to be near,

And 'gins to pale his uneffectual fire:

Adieu, adieu! Hamlet, remember me.

[handwritten note: King Hamlet tells Hamlet leave his mom to live with it.]

[Exit.]

Ham. *[handwritten note: ← Hamlet's second siliioquoy. Emotional × 10!]*

O all you host of heaven! O earth! what else?

And shall I couple hell? O, fie! – Hold, my heart;

And you, my sinews, grow not instant old,

But bear me stiffly up. – Remember thee!

Ay, thou poor ghost, while memory holds a seat

[handwritten note: The whole universe has put the despair and overwhelmed feeling on him.]

In this distracted globe. Remember thee! *melancholy feeling*

Yea, from the table of my memory

I'll wipe away all trivial fond records,

All saws of books, all forms, all pressures past, *Hamlet feels vengeful and he wants to let go of his past.*

That youth and observation copied there;

And thy commandment all alone shall live

Within the book and volume of my brain,

Unmix'd with baser matter: yes, by heaven! –

O most (pernicious) woman! → *wicked.* *He's mad at Gertrude. (hatred)*

O villain, villain, smiling, damned villain!

My tables, – meet it is I set it down, *He is feeling insane.*

That one may smile, and smile, and be a villain; *Hamlet does not know what to do.*

At least, I am sure, it may be so in Denmark:

[Writing.] ← *CONVICTION, DETERMINED*

So, uncle, there you are. Now to my word;

It is 'Adieu, adieu! remember me:'

I have sworn't.

Hor.

[Within.] My lord, my lord, –

Mar.

[Within.] Lord Hamlet, –

Hor.

[Within.] Heaven secure him!

Ham.

So be it!

Mar.

[Within.] Illo, ho, ho, my lord!

Ham.

Hillo, ho, ho, boy! Come, bird, come.

[Enter Horatio and Marcellus.]

Mar.

How is't, my noble lord?

Hor.

What news, my lord?

Ham.

O, wonderful!

* Hamlet and Horatio are arguing over who should tell the news.

Hor.

Good my lord, tell it.

Ham.

No; you'll reveal it.

The ghost is real

Hor.

Not I, my lord, by heaven.

Mar.

Nor I, my lord.

Ham.

How say you then; would heart of man once think it? –

But you'll be secret?

Hor. and Mar.

Ay, by heaven, my lord.

Ham.

There's ne'er a villain dwelling in all Denmark

But he's an arrant knave.

Hor.

There needs no ghost, my lord, come from the grave

To tell us this. ←———— Hamlet's Father (King Hamlet)

Ham.

Why, right; you are i' the right;

And so, without more circumstance at all,

I hold it fit that we shake hands and part:

You, as your business and desires shall point you, –

For every man hath business and desire,

Such as it is; – and for my own poor part,

Look you, I'll go pray.

Hamlet tells Marcellus the news of the ghost.

Hor.

These are but wild and whirling words, my lord.

Ham.

I'm sorry they offend you, heartily;

Yes, faith, heartily.

Hor.

There's no offence, my lord.

Ham.

Yes, by Saint Patrick, but there is, Horatio,

And much offence too. Touching this vision here, –

It is an honest ghost, that let me tell you:

For your desire to know what is between us,

O'ermaster't as you may. And now, good friends,

As you are friends, scholars, and soldiers,

Give me one poor request.

Hamlet asks of them not to tell anyone.

Hor.

What is't, my lord? we will.

Ham.

Never make known what you have seen to-night.

keep secret!

Hor. and Mar.

My lord, we will not.

Ham.

Nay, but swear't.

Hor.

In faith,

My lord, not I.

Mar.

Nor I, my lord, in faith.

lack of trust.

Ham.

Upon my sword.

Mar.

We have sworn, my lord, already.

Ham.

Indeed, upon my sword, indeed.

Ghost.

[Beneath.] Swear.

Ham.

Ha, ha boy! say'st thou so? art thou there, truepenny? –

Come on! – you hear this fellow in the cellarage, –

Consent to swear.

Hor.

Propose the oath, my lord.

Ham.

Never to speak of this that you have seen,

Swear by my sword.

Ghost.

[Beneath.] Swear.

Ham.

Hic et ubique? then we'll shift our ground. –

Come hither, gentlemen,

And lay your hands again upon my sword:

Never to speak of this that you have heard,

Swear by my sword.

Ghost.

[Beneath.] Swear.

Ham.

Well said, old mole! canst work i' the earth so fast?

A worthy pioner! – Once more remove, good friends.

Hor.

O day and night, but this is wondrous strange!

Ham.

And therefore as a stranger give it welcome.

There are more things in heaven and earth, Horatio, ⎤ *famous*
⎟ *quote.*
Than are dreamt of in your philosophy. ⎦

But come; —

Here, as before, never, so help you mercy,

How strange or odd soe'er I bear myself, —

As I, perchance, hereafter shall think meet

To put an antic disposition on, —

That you, at such times seeing me, never shall,

With arms encumber'd thus, or this head-shake,

Or by pronouncing of some doubtful phrase,

As 'Well, well, we know'; or 'We could, an if we would'; —

Or 'If we list to speak'; or 'There be, an if they might'; —

Or such ambiguous giving out, to note

That you know aught of me: — this is not to do,

So grace and mercy at your most need help you,

Swear.

Ghost.

[Beneath.] Swear.

There is so much going on besides what you are thinking.

Ham.

Rest, rest, perturbed spirit! – So, gentlemen,

With all my love I do commend me to you:

fore-shadowing
unbreakable bond.

And what so poor a man as Hamlet is

May do, to express his love and friending to you,

God willing, shall not lack. Let us go in together;

And still your fingers on your lips, I pray.

The time is out of joint: – O cursed spite,

tragedy (doomed)

That ever I was born to set it right! –

Nay, come, let's go together.

[Exeunt.]

Act II.

Scene I. A room in Polonius's house.

OBJ: what is its purpose?
. Polonius' personality → noisy
not a ~~villian~~ → distrustful
villain. caring.

→ Polonius's servant.

[Enter Polonius and Reynaldo.]

He's giving his servant. (He sends money in an envelope to Laertes in Paris.

Pol.

Give him this money and these notes, Reynaldo.

(Reynaldo) → He does not trust people in general. He is not very trusting.

Rey.

I will, my lord.

Pol.

You shall do marvellous wisely, good Reynaldo,

Before You visit him, to make inquiry

He wants him to check on Laertes.

Of his behaviour.

Rey.

My lord, I did intend it.

Pol.

Marry, well said; very well said. Look you, sir,

Enquire me first what Danskers are in Paris;

And how, and who, what means, and where they keep,

What company, at what expense; and finding,

By this encompassment and drift of question,

That they do know my son, come you more nearer

Than your particular demands will touch it:

Take you, as 'twere, some distant knowledge of him;

As thus, 'I know his father and his friends,

And in part him; – do you mark this, Reynaldo?

Rey.

Ay, very well, my lord.

Pol.

'And in part him; – but,' you may say, 'not well:

But if't be he I mean, he's very wild;

Addicted so and so;' and there put on him

What forgeries you please; marry, none so rank

As may dishonour him; take heed of that;

But, sir, such wanton, wild, and usual slips

Handwritten margin notes: He wants to know what Laertes want. investigation

*He basically wants him to investigate Laertes.

As are companions noted and most known

To youth and liberty.

He wants
Reynaldo to
~~me~~ meet others
and have them
tell Reynaldo ~~that~~
what he's up to
(making up stories.)

Rey.

— gambling

As gaming, my lord.

gambling

*there is a
lack of trust.

Pol.

Ay, or drinking, fencing, swearing, quarrelling, ←— On purpose

Drabbing: – you may go so far.

Rey.

My lord, that would dishonour him.

Pol.

Faith, no; as you may season it in the charge.

You must not put another scandal on him,

That he is open to incontinency;

That's not my meaning: but breathe his faults so quaintly

That they may seem the taints of liberty;

The flash and outbreak of a fiery mind;

A savageness in unreclaimed blood,

Of general assault.

Rey.

But, my good lord, –

Pol.

Wherefore should you do this?

Rey.

Ay, my lord,

I would know that.

Pol.

Marry, sir, here's my drift;

And I believe it is a fetch of warrant:

You laying these slight sullies on my son

As 'twere a thing a little soil'd i' the working,

Tells Reynaldo to check on him.

Mark you,

Your party in converse, him you would sound,

Having ever seen in the prenominate crimes

The youth you breathe of guilty, be assur'd

He closes with you in this consequence;

'Good sir,' or so; or 'friend,' or 'gentleman' –

According to the phrase or the addition

Of man and country.

Rey.

Very good, my lord.

*[handwritten: * creates a "mystery appeal" ind. opinion of Ophelia + her portrays an (old man) . the strong bond between father + mother]*

[handwritten: shakespeare does it on purpose. "history"! Polonius has no idea what he's saying. getting old]

Pol.

And then, sir, does he this, – he does – What was I about to say? –

By the mass, I was about to say something: – Where did I leave?

Rey.

At 'closes in the consequence,' at 'friend or so,' and

gentleman.'

[handwritten: Reynaldo agrees to do it!]

Pol.

At – closes in the consequence' – ay, marry!

He closes with you thus: – 'I know the gentleman;

I saw him yesterday, or t'other day, ← *[handwritten: talking about Laertes.]*

Or then, or then; with such, or such; and, as you say,

gambling

There was he gaming; there o'ertook in's rouse;

perhaps

There falling out at tennis': or perchance,

'I saw him enter such a house of sale,' –

Videlicet, a brothel, – or so forth. –

See you now;

Your bait of falsehood takes this carp of truth:

And thus do we of wisdom and of reach,

With windlaces, and with assays of bias,

By indirections find directions out:

So, by my former lecture and advice,

Shall you my son. You have me, have you not?

Rey.

My lord, I have.

Pol.

God b' wi' you, fare you well.

Rey.

Good my lord!

Pol.

Observe his inclination in yourself.

Rey.

I shall, my lord.

Pol.

And let him ply his music. ←——— talking about Laertes. ☺

Rey.

Well, my lord.

Pol.

Farewell!

[Exit Reynaldo.]

[Enter Ophelia.]

How now, Ophelia! what's the matter?

Oph.

scared out of her mind

Alas, my lord, I have been so affrighted! → *with Hamlet*

Pol.

With what, i' the name of God?

Oph.

My lord, as I was sewing in my chamber,

Lord Hamlet, – with his doublet all unbrac'd;

No hat upon his head; his stockings foul'd,

Ungart'red, and down-gyved to his ankle;

Pale as his shirt; his knees knocking each other;

And with a look so piteous in purport

As if he had been loosed out of hell

To speak of horrors, – he comes before me.

Hamle

she talks about her encounter with Hamlet and what had happened. Hamlet begins to act crazy!!!

Pol.

Mad for thy love? ← *is he mad for love?*

Oph.

My lord, I do not know;

But truly I do fear it.

Pol.

What said he?

Oph.

He took me by the wrist, and held me hard;

Then goes he to the length of all his arm;

And with his other hand thus o'er his brow,

He falls to such perusal of my face

As he would draw it. Long stay'd he so;

At last, – a little shaking of mine arm,

And thrice his head thus waving up and down, –

He rais'd a sigh so piteous and profound

As it did seem to shatter all his bulk

And end his being: that done, he lets me go:

And, with his head over his shoulder turn'd

He seem'd to find his way without his eyes;

For out o' doors he went without their help,

And to the last bended their light on me.

[Handwritten annotations:]

what Hamlet did to Ophelia.

* Ophelia describes how differently Hamlet acted towards her.

* Hamlet starts to act "crazy" and different.

* Hamlet looks pale and acts crazy.

← He let her go...

→ blinded.
← He did not look her in the eye.

Pol.

Pol. thinks its because Hamlet is overwrought.

Come, go with me: I will go seek the king.

This is the very ecstasy of love; *← Hamlet is acting violent.*

Whose violent property fordoes itself,

And leads the will to desperate undertakings,

As oft as any passion under heaven

That does afflict our natures. I am sorry, –

What, have you given him any hard words of late?

Any word to Hamlet lately?

Oph.

No, my good lord; but, as you did command,

I did repel his letters and denied

His access to me.

she denied his letters.

Pol.

That hath made him mad. *← mad "insane, crazy"*

I am sorry that with better heed and judgment

I had not quoted him: I fear'd he did but trifle,

(Hamlet)

And meant to wreck thee; but beshrew my jealousy! *← He is jealous*

It seems it as proper to our age

To cast beyond ourselves in our opinions

As it is common for the younger sort

To lack discretion. Come, go we to the king:

This must be known; which, being kept close, might move

More grief to hide than hate to utter love.

[Exeunt.]

Handwritten annotations:
Polonius feels guilty.

✗ Polonius feels concerned for Ophelia and apolegetic.

✳ Maybe Hamlet really loves her???

✳ Polonius wants to make it known. He's not a bad guy. He is naive. He's no villian.

Scene II. A room in the Castle.

[Enter King, Rosencrantz, Guildenstern, and Attendants.]

King.

Welcome, dear Rosencrantz and Guildenstern!

Moreover that we much did long to see you,

The need we have to use you did provoke

Our hasty sending. Something have you heard

Of Hamlet's transformation; so I call it,

Since nor the exterior nor the inward man

Resembles that it was. What it should be,

Handwritten annotations:
→ Claudius
Hamlet's second friend.
Hamlet's friend from school.
Hamlet's friend from school.
(Section 1)

Claudius wants Rosencrantz and Guildenstern to spy on Hamlet and tell him how he was acting.

Claudius

More than his father's death, that thus hath put him

So much from the understanding of himself,

I cannot dream of: I entreat you both

That, being of so young days brought up with him,

And since so neighbour'd to his youth and humour,

That you vouchsafe your rest here in our court

Some little time: so by your companies

To draw him on to pleasures, and to gather,

So much as from occasion you may glean,

Whether aught, to us unknown, afflicts him thus,

That, open'd, lies within our remedy.

King Claudius tells Rose Rosencrantz and Guildenstern about the way Hamlet has been acting.

Queen.   *King +*

Good gentlemen, he hath much talk'd of you,

And sure I am two men there are not living

To whom he more adheres. If it will please you

To show us so much gentry and good-will

As to expend your time with us awhile,

For the supply and profit of our hope,

Your visitation shall receive such thanks

As fits a king's remembrance.

Ros.

Both your majesties

Might, by the sovereign power you have of us,

Put your dread pleasures more into command

Than to entreaty.

Guil.

We both obey,

And here give up ourselves, in the full bent,

To lay our service freely at your feet,

To be commanded.

King.

Thanks, Rosencrantz and gentle Guildenstern.

Queen.

Thanks, Guildenstern and gentle Rosencrantz:

And I beseech you instantly to visit

My too-much-changed son. – Go, some of you,

And bring these gentlemen where Hamlet is.

*The king and Queen want R+G to cheer Hamlet up.

.The king really wants them to spy on Hamlet!

foreshadowing

.R+G are really dumb.

.They'll speak at the same time.

* They'll never respond to anything themselves.

Guil.

Heavens make our presence and our practices

Pleasant and helpful to him!

Queen.

Ay, amen!

[Exeunt Rosencrantz, Guildenstern, and some Attendants].

[Enter Polonius.]

Pol.

Th' ambassadors from Norway, my good lord,

Are joyfully return'd.

King.

Thou still hast been the father of good news.

Pol.

Have I, my lord? Assure you, my good liege,

I hold my duty, as I hold my soul,

Both to my God and to my gracious king:

[handwritten: voltimand is loyal (100%.)]

And I do think, – or else this brain of mine

Hunts not the trail of policy so sure

As it hath us'd to do, – that I have found

The very cause of Hamlet's lunacy.

King. _[handwritten: Claudius]_

O, speak of that; that do I long to hear.

Pol.

Give first admittance to the ambassadors;

My news shall be the fruit to that great feast.

King.

Thyself do grace to them, and bring them in.

[Exit Polonius.]

He tells me, my sweet queen, he hath found

The head and source of all your son's distemper.

Queen.

I doubt it is no other but the main, –

His father's death and our o'erhasty marriage.

King.

Well, we shall sift him.

[Enter Polonius, with Voltimand and Cornelius.]

Welcome, my good friends!

Say, Voltimand, what from our brother Norway?

Volt. ← ambassadors   assistants?

Most fair return of greetings and desires.

Upon our first, he sent out to suppress

His nephew's levies; which to him appear'd

To be a preparation 'gainst the Polack;

But, better look'd into, he truly found

It was against your highness; whereat griev'd, –

That so his sickness, age, and impotence

Was falsely borne in hand, – sends out arrests

He sends people to stop the conflict.

On Fortinbras; which he, in brief, obeys;

Receives rebuke from Norway; and, in fine,

war between N

Makes vow before his uncle never more

To give th' assay of arms against your majesty.

Whereon old Norway, overcome with joy,

Gives him three thousand crowns in annual fee;

They've gotten Fortinbras and now he has money to arm up against Poland.

And his commission to employ those soldiers,

So levied as before, against the Polack:

With an entreaty, herein further shown,

[Gives a paper.]

That it might please you to give quiet pass

Through your dominions for this enterprise,

On such regards of safety and allowance

As therein are set down.

King.

It likes us well;

And at our more consider'd time we'll read,

Claudius says: "I'll get back to you."

Answer, and think upon this business.

Meantime we thank you for your well-took labour:

Go to your rest; at night we'll feast together:

Most welcome home!

[Exeunt Voltimand and Cornelius.]

Pol.

This business is well ended. –

My liege, and madam, – to expostulate

What majesty should be, what duty is,

Why day is day, night is night, and time is time.

Were nothing but to waste night, day, and time.

Therefore, "since brevity is the soul of wit, " ← —— Pol.   → pure irony.

And tediousness the limbs and outward flourishes,

I will be brief: – your noble son is mad:

Mad call I it; for to define true madness,

What is't but to be nothing else but mad?

But let that go.

Queen.

More matter, with less art. ← she is sick of hearing it.

Pol.

Madam, I swear I use no art at all.

That he is mad, 'tis true: 'tis true 'tis pity; ← — Hamlet is mad.... ←

And pity 'tis 'tis true: a foolish figure;

But farewell it, for I will use no art.

Mad let us grant him then: and now remains

That we find out the cause of this effect;

Or rather say, the cause of this defect,

For this effect defective comes by cause:

Thus it remains, and the remainder thus.

Perpend. Ophelia

I have a daughter, – have whilst she is mine, – ⎤ Polonius is reading

Who, in her duty and obedience, mark, ⎟ Hamlet's love letter

Hath given me this: now gather, and surmise. ⎦ to Ophelia to the queen.

[Reads.]

'To the celestial, and my soul's idol, the most beautified

Ophelia,' –

That's an ill phrase, a vile phrase; 'beautified' is a vile

phrase: but you shall hear. Thus:

[Reads.]

'In her excellent white bosom, these, &c.'

Queen.

Came this from Hamlet to her?

Pol.

Good madam, stay awhile; I will be faithful.

[Reads.]

　'Doubt thou the stars are fire;

　　Doubt that the sun doth move;

　Doubt truth to be a liar;

　　But never doubt I love.

'O dear Ophelia, I am ill at these numbers; I have not art to

reckon my groans: but that I love thee best, O most best, believe

it. Adieu.

　'Thine evermore, most dear lady, whilst this machine is to him,

　　HAMLET.'

This, in obedience, hath my daughter show'd me;

And more above, hath his solicitings,

As they fell out by time, by means, and place,

All given to mine ear.

King.

But how hath she
Receiv'd his love?

Pol.

What do you think of me? ← — *Do you think I'd lie to you...?*

King.

As of a man faithful and honourable.

Pol.

I would fain prove so. But what might you think,

When I had seen this hot love on the wing, –

As I perceiv'd it, I must tell you that,

Before my daughter told me, – what might you,

when he found out, he saw it as lust.

Or my dear majesty your queen here, think,

If I had play'd the desk or table-book,

Or given my heart a winking, mute and dumb;

Or look'd upon this love with idle sight; –

What might you think? No, I went round to work,

And my young mistress thus I did bespeak:

'Lord Hamlet is a prince, out of thy sphere;

This must not be:' and then I precepts gave her,

That she should lock herself from his resort,

Admit no messengers, receive no tokens.

Which done, she took the fruits of my advice;

And he, repulsed, – a short tale to make, –

Fell into a sadness; then into a fast;

Thence to a watch; thence into a weakness;

Thence to a lightness; and, by this declension,

Into the madness wherein now he raves,

And all we wail for.

King.

Do you think 'tis this?

Queen.

It may be, very likely.

Pol.

Hath there been such a time, – I'd fain know that –

That I have positively said ''Tis so,'

When it prov'd otherwise?

King.

Not that I know.

Pol.

Take this from this, if this be otherwise:

[Points to his head and shoulder.]

If circumstances lead me, I will find

Where truth is hid, though it were hid indeed

Within the centre.

King.

How may we try it further?

Pol.

You know sometimes he walks for hours together

Here in the lobby.

Queen.

So he does indeed.

Pol.

At such a time I'll loose my daughter to him:

Be you and I behind an arras then;

Mark the encounter: if he love her not,

And he not from his reason fall'n thereon

Let me be no assistant for a state,

But keep a farm and carters.

creates a mystery.

Hamlet should...?

King.

We will try it.

Queen.

But look where sadly the poor wretch comes reading.

Pol.

Away, I do beseech you, both away

I'll board him presently: – O, give me leave.

[Exeunt King, Queen, and Attendants.]

[Enter Hamlet, reading.] ← ⟨Section 2⟩

How does my good Lord Hamlet? ← *What idea does he have?*

Ham.

Well, God-a-mercy.

* Polonius hides behind a tapastry.

* Hamlet still acts silly.

Pol.

Do you know me, my lord? ―

* Hamlet is babbling.

Ham.

Excellent well; you're a fishmonger.

ans – tapastry.
Polonius hides behind ~~besides~~ the tapastry, and listens in. He tests Ophelia.

Pol.

Not I, my lord.

Ham.

Then I would you were so honest a man.

Pol.

Honest, my lord!

Ham.

Ay, sir; to be honest, as this world goes, is to be one man

picked out of ten thousand.

Pol.

That's very true, my lord.

Ham.

For if the sun breed maggots in a dead dog, being a god-kissing

carrion, – Have you a daughter?

Pol.

I have, my lord. ←— Ophelia.

Ham.

Let her not walk i' the sun: conception is a blessing, but not

as your daughter may conceive: – friend, look to't.

Pol.

How say you by that? – [Aside.] Still harping on my daughter: – yet he knew me not at first; he said I was a fishmonger: he is far

gone, far gone: and truly in my youth I suffered much extremity

for love; very near this. I'll speak to him again. – What do you

read, my lord?

Ham.

Words, words, words.

throughout the whole thing, Hamlet is being very sarcastic. Hamlet is messing with Polonius.

Pol.

What is the matter, my lord?

Ham.

Between who?

Pol.

I mean, the matter that you read, my lord.

Ham.

Slanders, sir: for the satirical slave says here that old men

have grey beards; that their faces are wrinkled; their eyes

purging thick amber and plum-tree gum; and that they have a

plentiful lack of wit, together with most weak hams: all which,

sir, though I most powerfully and potently believe, yet I hold it

not honesty to have it thus set down; for you yourself, sir,

should be old as I am, if, like a crab, you could go backward.

Pol.

[Aside.] Though this be madness, yet there is a method in't. –

Will you walk out of the air, my lord? ←——— Polonius is talking to himself.

Are you responding in a certain way?

Ham.

Into my grave?

Pol.

Indeed, that is out o' the air. [Aside.] How pregnant sometimes

his replies are! a happiness that often madness hits on, which

reason and sanity could not so prosperously be delivered of. I

will leave him and suddenly contrive the means of meeting between

him and my daughter. – My honourable lord, I will most humbly take

my leave of you.

Ham.

You cannot, sir, take from me anything that I will more

willingly part withal, – except my life, except my life, except my

life.

Hamlet continues to act crazy.

Pol.

Fare you well, my lord.

Ham.

These tedious old fools!

[Enter Rosencrantz and Guildenstern.]

Pol.

You go to seek the Lord Hamlet; there he is.

Ros.

[To Polonius.] God save you, sir!

[Exit Polonius.] ← *Section 3*

Guil. ←— *acts dumb*

My honoured lord!

there is uncertainty in what Hamlet is saying.

Ros. ←— *acts dumb*

My most dear lord!

Ham.

My excellent good friends! How dost thou, Guildenstern? Ah,

Rosencrantz! Good lads, how do ye both?

Ros.

As the indifferent children of the earth.

Guil.

Happy in that we are not over-happy;

On fortune's cap we are not the very button.

Ham.

Nor the soles of her shoe?

Ros.

Neither, my lord.

Ham.

Then you live about her waist, or in the middle of her

favours?

Guil.

Faith, her privates we.

Ham.

In the secret parts of fortune? O, most true; she is a

strumpet. (What's the news?) ←——— what's up?

Ros.

None, my lord, but that the world's grown honest. ←——— they (R+G)
won't
answer
him

Ham.

Then is doomsday near; but your news is not true. Let me   he's
asking
to
question more in particular: what have you, my good friends,   tell
him again
deserved at the hands of fortune, that she sends you to (prison) → metaph
or
hither? ← whom can he trust.   " constantl
being
watched

Guil.

Prison, my lord!

Ham.

Denmark's a prison.

Ros.

Then is the world one.

Ham.

A goodly one; in which there are many confines, wards, and dungeons, Denmark being one o' the worst.

Ros.

We think not so, my lord.

Ham.

Why, then 'tis none to you; for there is nothing either good or bad but thinking makes it so: to me it is a prison.

Ros.

Why, then, your ambition makes it one; 'tis too narrow for your

mind.

Ham.

O God, I could be bounded in a nutshell, and count myself a

king of infinite space, were it not that I have bad dreams.

Guil.

Which dreams, indeed, are ambition; for the very substance of

the ambitious is merely the shadow of a dream.

Ham.

A dream itself is but a shadow. ⟵ Ham. says to Rosencrantz

Ros.

Truly, and I hold ambition of so airy and light a quality that

it is but a shadow's shadow.

Ham.

Then are our beggars bodies, and our monarchs and outstretch'd heroes the beggars' shadows. Shall we to the court? for, by my fay, I cannot reason.

Ros. and Guild.

We'll wait upon you. ←— *they talk together.*

Ham.

No such matter: I will not sort you with the rest of my servants; for, to speak to you like an honest man, I am most dreadfully attended. But, in the beaten way of friendship, what make you at Elsinore? ←— *this is the last time that he's asking "why they're here.*

Ros.

To visit you, my lord; no other occasion.

Ham.

Beggar that I am, I am even poor in thanks; but I thank you: and sure, dear friends, my thanks are too dear a halfpenny. Were you not sent for? Is it your own inclining? Is it a free visitation? Come, deal justly with me: come, come; nay, speak.

Hamlet is angry and he knows that he's lying to Hamlet.

Guil.

What should we say, my lord?

Ham.

Why, anything – but to the purpose. You were sent for; and

there is a kind of confession in your looks, which your modesties

have not craft enough to colour: I know the good king and queen

have sent for you. ← Hamlet knows that the queen and king have sent them there.

Ros.

To what end, my lord?

Ham.

That you must teach me. But let me conjure you, by the rights

of our fellowship, by the consonancy of our youth, by the

obligation of our ever-preserved love, and by what more dear a

better proposer could charge you withal, be even and direct with

me, whether you were sent for or no.

Ros.

[To Guildenstern.] What say you?

Ham.

[Aside.] Nay, then, I have an eye of you. – If you love me, hold

not off.

Guil.

My lord, we were sent for. ← — *Guildenstern finally reveals the truth. The key to them telling the truth, it does not help him.*

Ham.

I will tell you why; so shall my anticipation prevent your

discovery, and your secrecy to the king and queen moult no

feather. I have of late, – but wherefore I know not, – lost all my

mirth, forgone all custom of exercises; and indeed, it goes so

heavily with my disposition that this goodly frame, the earth, *Earth*

seems to me a sterile promontory; this most excellent canopy, the

air, look you, this brave o'erhanging firmament, this majestical

roof fretted with golden fire, – why, it appears no other thing

to me than a foul and pestilent congregation of vapours. What a

piece of work is man! How noble in reason! how infinite in

faculties! in form and moving, how express and admirable! in

action how like an angel! in apprehension, how like a god! the

Hamlet is describing the castle and everything

prison

everything

point where he's at.

beauty of the world! the paragon of animals! And yet, to me, what is this quintessence of dust? Man delights not me; no, nor woman neither, though by your smiling you seem to say so.

* everybody sucks.

Ros.

My lord, there was no such stuff in my thoughts.

← they ← (R+G) understand what he's thinking

Ham.

Why did you laugh then, when I said 'Man delights not me'?

Ros.

To think, my lord, if you delight not in man, what lenten entertainment the players shall receive from you: we coted them on the way; and hither are they coming to offer you service.

R+G tell him about the players

players about to cheer him up.

Ham.

common characters that people played at the time.

He that plays the king shall be welcome, – his majesty shall have tribute of me; the adventurous knight shall use his foil and target; the lover shall not sigh gratis; the humorous man shall end his part in peace; the clown shall make those laugh whose lungs are tickle o' the sere; and the lady shall say her mind

R+G mention the players and Hamlet decides to "capture" Claudius by having players enact King Hamlet's death.

freely, or the blank verse shall halt for't. What players are

they?

Ros.

Even those you were wont to take such delight in, – the

tragedians of the city. ⟵——— *the players perform tragedy.*

Ham.

How chances it they travel? their residence, both in

reputation and profit, was better both ways.

Ros.

I think their inhibition comes by the means of the late

innovation.

Ham.

Do they hold the same estimation they did when I was in the

city? Are they so followed?

Ros.

No, indeed, are they not.

Ham.

How comes it? do they grow rusty?

Ros.

[handwritten annotation: boys played the roles of women @ the time]

Nay, their endeavour keeps in the wonted pace: but there is,

sir, an aery of children, little eyases, that cry out on the top

of question, and are most tyrannically clapped for't: these are

now the fashion; and so berattle the common stages, – so they call

them, – that many wearing rapiers are afraid of goose-quills and

dare scarce come thither.

Ham.

What, are they children? who maintains 'em? How are they

escoted? Will they pursue the quality no longer than they can

sing? will they not say afterwards, if they should grow

themselves to common players, – as it is most like, if their means

are no better, – their writers do them wrong to make them exclaim

against their own succession?

Ros.

Faith, there has been much to do on both sides; and the nation

holds it no sin to tarre them to controversy: there was, for

awhile, no money bid for argument unless the poet and the player

went to cuffs in the question.

Ham.

Is't possible?

Guil.

O, there has been much throwing about of brains.

Ham.

Do the boys carry it away?

Ros.

Ay, that they do, my lord; Hercules and his load too.

reference to Globe theatre in London.

Ham.

It is not very strange; for my uncle is king of Denmark, and

those that would make mouths at him while my father lived, give

twenty, forty, fifty, a hundred ducats a-piece for his picture in

☆FORESHADOWING

little. 'Sblood, there is something in this more than natural, if

philosophy could find it out. ← — *Hamlet is planning to have the players peform a play that mimicks king Hamlet's tragic death.*

[Flourish of trumpets within.]

Guil.

There are the players. ← — *the players are here.*

Ham.

Gentlemen, you are welcome to Elsinore. Your hands, come: the

appurtenance of welcome is fashion and ceremony: let me comply

with you in this garb; lest my extent to the players, which I

tell you must show fairly outward, should more appear like

entertainment than yours. You are welcome: but my uncle-father

and aunt-mother are deceived.

↑ foreshadowing...   *They used to like him, but now they don't....*

Guil.

In what, my dear lord? ← *what is he saying.*

Ham.

I am but mad north-north-west: when the wind is southerly I

know a hawk from a handsaw. ⟵ *Right now they think he is mad, but he is not.*

. They will eventually tell the king.

[Enter Polonius.]

. It's obvious that is more clever.

Pol.

Well be with you, gentlemen!

Ham.

Hark you, Guildenstern; — and you too; — at each ear a hearer: that

great baby you see there is not yet out of his swaddling clouts.

Ros.

Happily he's the second time come to them; for they say an old

man is twice a child.

Ham.

I will prophesy he comes to tell me of the players; mark it. — You

say right, sir: o' Monday morning; 'twas so indeed.

Pol. ⟵ *Polonius goes on and on about this topic.*

My lord, I have news to tell you.

Ham.

My lord, I have news to tell you. When Roscius was an actor in

Rome, –

Pol.

The actors are come hither, my lord.

Ham.

Buzz, buzz!

Pol.

Upon my honour, –

Ham.

Then came each actor on his ass, –

Pol.

The best actors in the world, either for tragedy, comedy,

history, pastoral, pastoral-comical, historical-pastoral,

tragical-historical, tragical-comical-historical-pastoral, scene individable, or poem unlimited: Seneca cannot be too heavy nor

Plautus too light. For the law of writ and the liberty, these are

the only men.

Ham.

O Jephthah, judge of Israel, what a treasure hadst thou!

Pol.

What treasure had he, my lord?

Ham.

Why –

  'One fair daughter, and no more,

  The which he loved passing well.'

Pol.

[Aside.] Still on my daughter.

Ham.

Am I not i' the right, old Jephthah?

Pol.

If you call me Jephthah, my lord, I have a daughter that I

love passing well.

Ham.

Nay, that follows not.

It reiterates that Hamlet is better than all of them.

Pol.

What follows, then, my lord?

S

Ham.

Why –

  'As by lot, God wot,'

and then, you know,

  'It came to pass, as most like it was – '

* Hamlet is making a reference to a character.

The first row of the pious chanson will show you more; for look

where my abridgment comes.

Sili soliloquy!!!

* Hamlet asks the players if they can perform a play for him.

[Enter four or five Players.] ← (Section 4)

You are welcome, masters; welcome, all: – I am glad to see thee

well. – welcome, good friends. – O, my old friend! Thy face is

valanc'd since I saw thee last; comest thou to beard me in

Denmark? – What, my young lady and mistress! By'r lady, your

ladyship is nearer to heaven than when I saw you last, by the

altitude of a chopine. Pray God, your voice, like a piece of

uncurrent gold, be not cracked within the ring. – Masters, you are

all welcome. We'll e'en to't like French falconers, fly at

anything we see: we'll have a speech straight: come, give us a

taste of your quality: come, a passionate speech.

I Play.

What speech, my lord?

Ham.

I heard thee speak me a speech once, – but it was never acted;

or if it was, not above once; for the play, I remember, pleased

not the million, 'twas caviare to the general; but it was, – as I

received it, and others, whose judgments in such matters cried in

the top of mine, – an excellent play, well digested in the scenes,

set down with as much modesty as cunning. I remember, one said there were no sallets in the lines to make the matter savoury,

nor no matter in the phrase that might indite the author of

affectation; but called it an honest method, as wholesome as

sweet, and by very much more handsome than fine. One speech in it

I chiefly loved: 'twas AEneas' tale to Dido, and thereabout of it

especially where he speaks of Priam's slaughter: if it live in

your memory, begin at this line; – let me see, let me see: –

The rugged Pyrrhus, like th' Hyrcanian beast, –

it is not so: – it begins with Pyrrhus: –

'The rugged Pyrrhus, – he whose sable arms,

Black as his purpose, did the night resemble

When he lay couched in the ominous horse, –

Hath now this dread and black complexion smear'd

With heraldry more dismal; head to foot

Now is he total gules; horridly trick'd

With blood of fathers, mothers, daughters, sons,

Bak'd and impasted with the parching streets,

That lend a tyrannous and a damned light

To their vile murders: roasted in wrath and fire,

And thus o'ersized with coagulate gore,

With eyes like carbuncles, the hellish Pyrrhus

Old grandsire Priam seeks.'

So, proceed you.

Pol.

'Fore God, my lord, well spoken, with good accent and good

discretion.

I Play.

Anon he finds him,

Striking too short at Greeks: his antique sword,

Rebellious to his arm, lies where it falls,

Repugnant to command: unequal match'd,

Pyrrhus at Priam drives; in rage strikes wide;

But with the whiff and wind of his fell sword

The unnerved father falls. Then senseless Ilium,

Seeming to feel this blow, with flaming top

Stoops to his base; and with a hideous crash

Takes prisoner Pyrrhus' ear: for lo! his sword,

Which was declining on the milky head

Of reverend Priam, seem'd i' the air to stick:

So, as a painted tyrant, Pyrrhus stood;

And, like a neutral to his will and matter,

Did nothing.

But as we often see, against some storm,

A silence in the heavens, the rack stand still,

The bold winds speechless, and the orb below

As hush as death, anon the dreadful thunder

Doth rend the region; so, after Pyrrhus' pause,

A roused vengeance sets him new a-work;

And never did the Cyclops' hammers fall

On Mars's armour, forg'd for proof eterne,

With less remorse than Pyrrhus' bleeding sword

Now falls on Priam. –

Out, out, thou strumpet, Fortune! All you gods,

In general synod, take away her power;

Break all the spokes and fellies from her wheel,

And bowl the round nave down the hill of heaven,

As low as to the fiends!

Pol.

This is too long.

Ham.

It shall to the barber's, with your beard. – Pr'ythee say on. –

He's for a jig or a tale of bawdry, or he sleeps: – say on; come

to Hecuba.

I Play.

But who, O who, had seen the mobled queen, –

Ham.

'The mobled queen'?

Pol.

That's good! 'Mobled queen' is good.

I Play.

Run barefoot up and down, threatening the flames

With bisson rheum; a clout upon that head

Where late the diadem stood, and for a robe,

About her lank and all o'erteemed loins,

A blanket, in the alarm of fear caught up; –

Who this had seen, with tongue in venom steep'd,

'Gainst Fortune's state would treason have pronounc'd:

But if the gods themselves did see her then,

When she saw Pyrrhus make malicious sport

In mincing with his sword her husband's limbs,

The instant burst of clamour that she made, –

Unless things mortal move them not at all, –

Would have made milch the burning eyes of heaven,

And passion in the gods.

Pol.

Look, whether he has not turn'd his colour, and has tears in's

eyes. – Pray you, no more!

Ham.

'Tis well. I'll have thee speak out the rest of this soon. –

Good my lord, will you see the players well bestowed? Do you

hear? Let them be well used; for they are the abstracts and brief chronicles of the time; after your death you were better have a

bad epitaph than their ill report while you live.

Pol.

My lord, I will use them according to their desert.

Ham.

Odd's bodikin, man, better: use every man after his

desert, and who should scape whipping? Use them after your own

honour and dignity: the less they deserve, the more merit is in

your bounty. Take them in.

Pol.

Come, sirs.

Ham.

Follow him, friends: we'll hear a play to-morrow.

[Exeunt Polonius with all the Players but the First.]

Dost thou hear me, old friend? Can you play 'The Murder of

Gonzago'? ←

I Play.

Ay, my lord.

Ham.

We'll ha't to-morrow night. You could, for a need, study a

speech of some dozen or sixteen lines which I would set down and

insert in't? could you not?

> *Hamlet wants the players to act out his father's death to capture claudius.

I Play.

Ay, my lord.

Ham.

Very well. – Follow that lord; and look you mock him not.

[Exit First Player.]

 – My good friends [to Ros. and Guild.], I'll leave you till

night: you are welcome to Elsinore.

Ros.

Good my lord!

[Exeunt Rosencrantz and Guildenstern.] ← (Section 5)

Ham. ← Hamlet's 3rd Siliqoy.

Ay, so, God b' wi' ye!

* It tracks his emotional state.

Now I am alone.

* He is clearly thinking and he's realizing some things.

O, what a rogue and peasant slave am I!

Is it not monstrous that this player here,

But in a fiction, in a dream of passion,

Could force his soul so to his own conceit

Hamlet is saying that he's alone and

That from her working all his visage wan'd;

Tears in his eyes, distraction in's aspect,

A broken voice, and his whole function suiting

With forms to his conceit? And all for nothing!

For Hecuba?

What's Hecuba to him, or he to Hecuba,

Hamlet is realizing that, this is what he should be doing.

That he should weep for her? What would he do,

Had he the motive and the cue for passion

That I have? He would drown the stage with tears

And cleave the general ear with horrid speech;

Make mad the guilty, and appal the free;

Confound the ignorant, and amaze, indeed,

The very faculties of eyes and ears.

Yet I,

A dull and muddy-mettled rascal, peak,

Like John-a-dreams, unpregnant of my cause,

And can say nothing; no, not for a king

Upon whose property and most dear life

A damn'd defeat was made. Am I a coward?

Who calls me villain? breaks my pate across?

Plucks off my beard and blows it in my face?

Tweaks me by the nose? gives me the lie i' the throat

As deep as to the lungs? who does me this, ha?

'Swounds, I should take it: for it cannot be

But I am pigeon-liver'd, and lack gall

To make oppression bitter; or ere this

I should have fatted all the region kites

With this slave's offal: bloody, bawdy villain!

Remorseless, treacherous, lecherous, kindless villain!

O, vengeance!

He is being more specific

Hamlet

Why, what an ass am I! This is most brave,

That I, the son of a dear father murder'd,

Prompted to my revenge by heaven and hell,

Must, like a whore, unpack my heart with words

And fall a-cursing like a very drab,

A scullion! ← *lowest/peasant maid.*

Fie upon't! foh! – About, my brain! I have heard

That guilty creatures, sitting at a play,

someone watching a play reminds them of something.

Have by the very cunning of the scene

Been struck so to the soul that presently

They have proclaim'd their malefactions;

VOLTA LINE For murder, though it have no tongue, will speak

With most miraculous organ, I'll have these players

Play something like the murder of my father

Before mine uncle: I'll observe his looks;

I'll tent him to the quick: if he but blench,

I know my course. The spirit that I have seen

May be the devil: and the devil hath power

To assume a pleasing shape; yea, and perhaps

Out of my weakness and my melancholy, –

As he is very potent with such spirits, –

Hamlet is disgusted with himself.

He is calling himself "pathetic" and saying that he should do all of these things.

Abuses me to damn me: I'll have grounds

More relative than this. – the play's the thing

Wherein I'll catch the conscience of the king.

It tracks him.

[Exit.]

ACT III.

Scene I. A room in the Castle.

[Enter King, Queen, Polonius, Ophelia, Rosencrantz, and
Guildenstern.]

King. ← Claudius

And can you, by no drift of circumstance,

Get from him why he puts on this confusion,

Grating so harshly all his days of quiet

With turbulent and dangerous lunacy?

Ros.

He does confess he feels himself distracted,

But from what cause he will by no means speak.

Guil.

Nor do we find him forward to be sounded,

But, with a crafty madness, keeps aloof

When we would bring him on to some confession

Of his true state.

Queen. ←— *different claudius.

Did he receive you well?

Ros.

Most like a gentleman.

Guil.

But with much forcing of his disposition.

Ros.

Niggard of question; but, of our demands,

Most free in his reply.

Queen.

Did you assay him

To any pastime?

Ros.

Madam, it so fell out that certain players

We o'er-raught on the way: of these we told him,

And there did seem in him a kind of joy

To hear of it: they are about the court,

And, as I think, they have already order

This night to play before him.

Pol.

'Tis most true;

And he beseech'd me to entreat your majesties

To hear and see the matter.

King.

With all my heart; and it doth much content me

To hear him so inclin'd. –

Good gentlemen, give him a further edge,

And drive his purpose on to these delights.

Ros.

We shall, my lord.

[Exeunt Rosencrantz and Guildenstern.]

King.

Sweet Gertrude, leave us too;

For we have closely sent for Hamlet hither,

That he, as 'twere by accident, may here

Affront Ophelia:

Her father and myself, – lawful espials, –

Will so bestow ourselves that, seeing, unseen,

We may of their encounter frankly judge;

And gather by him, as he is behav'd,

If't be the affliction of his love or no

That thus he suffers for.

"worried about Hamlet".

Queen.

I shall obey you: –

And for your part, Ophelia, I do wish

That your good beauties be the happy cause

Of Hamlet's wildness: so shall I hope your virtues

Will bring him to his wonted way again,

To both your honours.

Oph.

Madam, I wish it may.

[Exit Queen.]

Pol.

Ophelia, walk you here. – Gracious, so please you,

We will bestow ourselves. – [To Ophelia.] Read on this book;

That show of such an exercise may colour

As Ophelia is just walking around we will watch her.

Your loneliness. – We are oft to blame in this, –

'Tis too much prov'd, – that with devotion's visage

And pious action we do sugar o'er

The Devil himself. *Ophelia lies to Hamlet*

King.

[Aside.] O, 'tis too true!

– has a talk to himself and the first time in the play, he has a guilty conscience

How smart a lash that speech doth give my conscience!

The harlot's cheek, beautied with plastering art,

Is not more ugly to the thing that helps it

Than is my deed to my most painted word:

O heavy burden!

Pol.

I hear him coming: let's withdraw, my lord.

[Exeunt King and Polonius.]

[Enter Hamlet.]

Ham. *— 4th soliloquy and it is the most famous. It is about mankind.*

To be, or not to be, – that is the question: –

Whether 'tis nobler in the mind to suffer

The slings and arrows of outrageous fortune

Or to take arms against a sea of troubles,

And by opposing end them? – To die, – to sleep, –

Hamlet finds out that Ophelia is watching him and discovers that she is lying

No more; and by a sleep to say we end

The heartache, and the thousand natural shocks

That flesh is heir to, – 'tis a consummation

Devoutly to be wish'd. To die, – to sleep; –

To sleep! perchance to dream: – ay, there's the rub;

For in that sleep of death what dreams may come,

mankind

When we have shuffled off this mortal coil, ⟶ *something that is wrapped around and won't let go.*

Must give us pause: there's the respect

That makes calamity of so long life;

For who would bear the whips and scorns of time,

The oppressor's wrong, the proud man's contumely,

The pangs of despis'd love, the law's delay,

The insolence of office, and the spurns

That patient merit of the unworthy takes,

When he himself might his quietus make

With a bare bodkin? who would these fardels bear,

To grunt and sweat under a weary life,

But that the dread of something after death, –

The undiscover'd country, from whose bourn

No traveller returns, – puzzles the will,

And makes us rather bear those ills we have

Than fly to others that we know not of?

Thus conscience does make cowards of us all;

And thus the native hue of resolution

Is sicklied o'er with the pale cast of thought;

And enterprises of great pith and moment,

With this regard, their currents turn awry,

And lose the name of action. – Soft you now!

Hamlet is saying that we'd rather do the one thing over the other.

The fair Ophelia! – Nymph, in thy orisons

Be all my sins remember'd.

Oph.

Good my lord,

How does your honour for this many a day?

Ham.

I humbly thank you; well, well, well.

Oph.

My lord, I have remembrances of yours

That I have longed long to re-deliver.

I pray you, now receive them.

Ophelia wants to give some stuff back.

Ham.

No, not I;

I never gave you aught.

Oph.

My honour'd lord, you know right well you did;

And with them words of so sweet breath compos'd

As made the things more rich; their perfume lost,

Take these again; for to the noble mind

Rich gifts wax poor when givers prove unkind.

There, my lord.

Ham.

Ha, ha! are you honest?

Oph.

My lord?

Ham.

Are you fair?

Oph.

What means your lordship?

Ham.

That if you be honest and fair, your honesty should admit no

discourse to your beauty.

Oph.

Could beauty, my lord, have better commerce than with honesty?

Ham.

Ay, truly; for the power of beauty will sooner transform

honesty from what it is to a bawd than the force of honesty can

translate beauty into his likeness: this was sometime a paradox,

but now the time gives it proof. I did love you once.

Oph.

Indeed, my lord, you made me believe so.

Ham.

You should not have believ'd me; for virtue cannot so

inoculate our old stock but we shall relish of it: I loved you

not.

Oph.

I was the more deceived.

Ham.

Get thee to a nunnery: why wouldst thou be a breeder of

sinners? I am myself indifferent honest; but yet I could accuse

me of such things that it were better my mother had not borne me:

I am very proud, revengeful, ambitious; with more offences at my

beck than I have thoughts to put them in, imagination to give

them shape, or time to act them in. What should such fellows as I

do crawling between earth and heaven? We are arrant knaves, all;

believe none of us. Go thy ways to a nunnery. Where's your

father?

Hamlet is talking about all men and says that they're all jerks.

Oph.

At home, my lord. *Hamlet discovers that Ophelia has just lied to him.*

Ham.

Let the doors be shut upon him, that he may play the fool

nowhere but in's own house. Farewell.

Oph.

O, help him, you sweet heavens!

Ham.

If thou dost marry, I'll give thee this plague for thy dowry, –

be thou as chaste as ice, as pure as snow, thou shalt not escape

calumny. Get thee to a nunnery, go: farewell. Or, if thou wilt

needs marry, marry a fool; for wise men know well enough what

monsters you make of them. To a nunnery, go; and quickly too.

Farewell.

Oph.

O heavenly powers, restore him!

Ham.

I have heard of your paintings too, well enough; God hath

given you one face, and you make yourselves another: you jig, you

amble, and you lisp, and nickname God's creatures, and make your

wantonness your ignorance. Go to, I'll no more on't; it hath made

me mad. I say, we will have no more marriages: those that are

married already, all but one, shall live; the rest shall keep as

they are. To a nunnery, go.

[Exit.]

Oph. — *her most famous speech, and talks about the old Hamlet and how he would've reacted if he wasn't angry*

O, what a noble mind is here o'erthrown!

The courtier's, scholar's, soldier's, eye, tongue, sword,

The expectancy and rose of the fair state,

The glass of fashion and the mould of form,

The observ'd of all observers, – quite, quite down!

And I, of ladies most deject and wretched

That suck'd the honey of his music vows,

Now see that noble and most sovereign reason,

Like sweet bells jangled, out of tune and harsh;

That unmatch'd form and feature of blown youth

Blasted with ecstasy: O, woe is me,

To have seen what I have seen, see what I see!

[Re-enter King and Polonius.] *the king is not sure what to think.*

King. *→ he thinks that something is not right.*

Love! his affections do not that way tend;

Nor what he spake, though it lack'd form a little,

Was not like madness. There's something in his soul

O'er which his melancholy sits on brood;

And I do doubt the hatch and the disclose

Will be some danger: which for to prevent,

I have in quick determination

Thus set it down: – he shall with speed to England *he ~~had~~ wants to go and get Hamlet*

For the demand of our neglected tribute: *money*

Haply the seas, and countries different,

With variable objects, shall expel

This something-settled matter in his heart;

Whereon his brains still beating puts him thus

From fashion of himself. What think you on't?

Pol. *His idea is to talk to Gertrude and spy on Hamlet.*

It shall do well: but yet do I believe

The origin and commencement of his grief

Sprung from neglected love. – How now, Ophelia!

You need not tell us what Lord Hamlet said;

We heard it all. – My lord, do as you please;

But if you hold it fit, after the play,

Let his queen mother all alone entreat him

To show his grief: let her be round with him;

And I'll be plac'd, so please you, in the ear ← *another pun.*

Of all their conference. If she find him not,

To England send him; or confine him where

Your wisdom best shall think.

King.

It shall be so:

Madness in great ones must not unwatch'd go.

The king says.

[Exeunt.]

Scene II. A hall in the Castle.

[Enter Hamlet and certain Players.]

Ham.

Speak the speech, I pray you, as I pronounced it to you,

trippingly on the tongue: but if you mouth it, as many of your

players do, I had as lief the town crier spoke my lines. Nor do not saw the air too much with your hand, thus, but use all

gently: for in the very torrent, tempest, and, as I may say,

whirlwind of passion, you must acquire and beget a

temperance that may give it smoothness. O, it offends me to the

soul, to hear a robustious periwig-pated fellow tear a passion to

tatters, to very rags, to split the ears of the groundlings, who,

for the most part, are capable of nothing but inexplicable dumb

shows and noise: I would have such a fellow whipped for o'erdoing

Termagant; it out-herods Herod: pray you avoid it.

I Player.

I warrant your honour.

Ham.

Be not too tame neither; but let your own discretion be your

tutor: suit the action to the word, the word to the action; with

this special observance, that you o'erstep not the modesty of

nature: for anything so overdone is from the purpose of playing,

whose end, both at the first and now, was and is, to hold, as

'twere, the mirror up to nature; to show virtue her own image,

scorn her own image, and the very age and body of the time his form and pressure. Now, this overdone, or come tardy off, though it make the unskilful laugh, cannot but make the judicious grieve; the censure of the which one must in your allowance, o'erweigh a whole theatre of others. O, there be players that I have seen play, – and heard others praise, and that highly, – not to speak it profanely, that, neither having the accent of Christians, nor the gait of Christian, pagan, nor man, have so strutted and bellowed that I have thought some of nature's journeymen had made men, and not made them well, they imitated humanity so abominably.

I Player.

I hope we have reform'd that indifferently with us, sir.

Ham.

O, reform it altogether. And let those that play your clowns speak no more than is set down for them: for there be of them that will themselves laugh, to set on some quantity of barren spectators to laugh too, though in the meantime some necessary question of the play be then to be considered: that's villanous and shows a most pitiful ambition in the fool that uses it. Go make you ready.

[Exeunt Players.]

[Enter Polonius, Rosencrantz, and Guildenstern.]

How now, my lord! will the king hear this piece of work?

Pol.

And the queen too, and that presently.

Ham.

Bid the players make haste.

[Exit Polonius.]

Will you two help to hasten them?

Ros. and Guil.

We will, my lord.

[Exeunt Ros. and Guil.]

Ham.

What, ho, Horatio!

[Enter Horatio.]

Hor.

Here, sweet lord, at your service.

Ham.

Horatio, thou art e'en as just a man

As e'er my conversation cop'd withal.

Hor.

O, my dear lord, –

Ham.

Nay, do not think I flatter;

For what advancement may I hope from thee,

That no revenue hast, but thy good spirits,

To feed and clothe thee? Why should the poor be flatter'd?

No, let the candied tongue lick absurd pomp;

And crook the pregnant hinges of the knee

Where thrift may follow fawning. Dost thou hear?

Since my dear soul was mistress of her choice,

And could of men distinguish, her election

Hath seal'd thee for herself: for thou hast been

As one, in suffering all, that suffers nothing;

A man that Fortune's buffets and rewards

Hast ta'en with equal thanks: and bles'd are those

Whose blood and judgment are so well commingled

That they are not a pipe for Fortune's finger

To sound what stop she please. Give me that man

That is not passion's slave, and I will wear him

In my heart's core, ay, in my heart of heart,

As I do thee. – Something too much of this. –

There is a play to-night before the king;

One scene of it comes near the circumstance,

Which I have told thee, of my father's death:

I pr'ythee, when thou see'st that act a-foot,

Even with the very comment of thy soul

[Handwritten margin note: Everyone at this point has either lied to him or died even.]

[Handwritten margin note: Hamlet explains to Horatio what the play is exactly about.]

Observe mine uncle: if his occulted guilt

Do not itself unkennel in one speech,

It is a damned ghost that we have seen;

And my imaginations are as foul

As Vulcan's stithy. Give him heedful note;

For I mine eyes will rivet to his face;

And, after, we will both our judgments join

In censure of his seeming.

Hor.

Well, my lord:

If he steal aught the whilst this play is playing,

And scape detecting, I will pay the theft.

Ham.

They are coming to the play. I must be idle:

Get you a place.

[Danish march. A flourish. Enter King, Queen, Polonius, Ophelia,

Rosencrantz, Guildenstern, and others.]

King.

How fares our cousin Hamlet?

Ham.

Excellent, i' faith; of the chameleon's dish: I eat the air, promise-crammed: you cannot feed capons so.

King.

I have nothing with this answer, Hamlet; these words are not mine.

Ham.

No, nor mine now. My lord, you play'd once i' the university, you say? [To Polonius.]

Pol.

That did I, my lord, and was accounted a good actor.

Ham.

What did you enact?

Pol.

I did enact Julius Caesar; I was kill'd i' the Capitol; Brutus

killed me. ← *Shakespeare loves to refer to his Roman characters.*

Ham.

It was a brute part of him to kill so capital a calf there. – Be

the players ready? *Hamlet is being naughty and*

Ros.

Ay, my lord; they stay upon your patience.

Queen.

Come hither, my dear Hamlet, sit by me.

Ham.

No, good mother, here's metal more attractive.

Pol.

O, ho! do you mark that? [To the King.]

Ham.

Lady, shall I lie in your lap?

[Lying down at Ophelia's feet.]

Oph.

No, my lord.

Ham.

I mean, my head upon your lap?

Hamlet is being naughty with Ha. Ophelia.

Oph.

Ay, my lord.

Ham.

Do you think I meant country matters?

Oph.

I think nothing, my lord.

Ham.

That's a fair thought to lie between maids' legs.

Oph.

What is, my lord?

Ham.

Nothing.

Oph.

You are merry, my lord.

Ham.

Who, I?

Oph.

Ay, my lord.

Ham.

O, your only jig-maker! What should a man do but be merry?
for look you how cheerfully my mother looks, and my father died
within 's two hours.

Oph.

Nay, 'tis twice two months, my lord.

Ham.

So long? Nay then, let the devil wear black, for I'll have a

suit of sables. O heavens! die two months ago, and not forgotten

yet? Then there's hope a great man's memory may outlive his life

half a year: but, by'r lady, he must build churches then; or else

shall he suffer not thinking on, with the hobby-horse, whose

epitaph is 'For, O, for, O, the hobby-horse is forgot!'

[Trumpets sound. The dumb show enters.]

[Enter a King and a Queen very lovingly; the Queen embracing

him and he her. She kneels, and makes show of protestation

unto him. He takes her up, and declines his head upon her

neck: lays him down upon a bank of flowers: she, seeing

him asleep, leaves him. Anon comes in a fellow, takes off his

crown, kisses it, pours poison in the king's ears, and exit. The

Queen returns, finds the King dead, and makes passionate action.

The Poisoner with some three or four Mutes, comes in again,

seeming to lament with her. The dead body is carried away. The

Poisoner wooes the Queen with gifts; she seems loth and unwilling awhile, but in the end accepts his love.]

[Exeunt.]

Oph.

What means this, my lord?

Ham.

Marry, this is miching mallecho; it means mischief.

Oph.

Belike this show imports the argument of the play.

[Enter Prologue.]

Ham.

We shall know by this fellow: the players cannot keep counsel; they'll tell all.

Oph.

Will he tell us what this show meant?

Ham.

Ay, or any show that you'll show him: be not you ashamed to

show, he'll not shame to tell you what it means.

Oph.

You are naught, you are naught: I'll mark the play.

Pro.

   For us, and for our tragedy,

   Here stooping to your clemency,

   We beg your hearing patiently.

Ham.

Is this a prologue, or the posy of a ring?

Oph.

'Tis brief, my lord.

Ham.

As woman's love.

[Enter a King and a Queen.]

P. King.

Full thirty times hath Phoebus' cart gone round

Neptune's salt wash and Tellus' orbed ground,

And thirty dozen moons with borrow'd sheen

About the world have times twelve thirties been,

Since love our hearts, and Hymen did our hands,

Unite commutual in most sacred bands.

P. Queen.

So many journeys may the sun and moon

Make us again count o'er ere love be done!

But, woe is me, you are so sick of late,

So far from cheer and from your former state.

That I distrust you. Yet, though I distrust,

Discomfort you, my lord, it nothing must:

For women's fear and love holds quantity;

In neither aught, or in extremity.

Now, what my love is, proof hath made you know;

And as my love is siz'd, my fear is so:

Where love is great, the littlest doubts are fear;

Where little fears grow great, great love grows there.

P. King.

Faith, I must leave thee, love, and shortly too;

My operant powers their functions leave to do:

And thou shalt live in this fair world behind,

Honour'd, belov'd, and haply one as kind

For husband shalt thou, –

P. Queen.

O, confound the rest!

Such love must needs be treason in my breast:

In second husband let me be accurst!

None wed the second but who kill'd the first.

Ham.

[Aside.] Wormwood, wormwood!

P. Queen.

The instances that second marriage move

Are base respects of thrift, but none of love.

A second time I kill my husband dead

When second husband kisses me in bed.

P. King.

I do believe you think what now you speak;

But what we do determine oft we break.

Purpose is but the slave to memory;

Of violent birth, but poor validity:

Which now, like fruit unripe, sticks on the tree;

But fall unshaken when they mellow be.

Most necessary 'tis that we forget

To pay ourselves what to ourselves is debt:

What to ourselves in passion we propose,

The passion ending, doth the purpose lose.

The violence of either grief or joy

Their own enactures with themselves destroy:

Where joy most revels, grief doth most lament;

Grief joys, joy grieves, on slender accident.

This world is not for aye; nor 'tis not strange

That even our loves should with our fortunes change;

For 'tis a question left us yet to prove,

Whether love lead fortune, or else fortune love.

The great man down, you mark his favourite flies,

The poor advanc'd makes friends of enemies;

And hitherto doth love on fortune tend:

For who not needs shall never lack a friend;

And who in want a hollow friend doth try,

Directly seasons him his enemy.

But, orderly to end where I begun, –

Our wills and fates do so contrary run

That our devices still are overthrown;

Our thoughts are ours, their ends none of our own:

So think thou wilt no second husband wed;

But die thy thoughts when thy first lord is dead.

P. Queen.

Nor earth to me give food, nor heaven light!

Sport and repose lock from me day and night!

To desperation turn my trust and hope!

An anchor's cheer in prison be my scope!

Each opposite that blanks the face of joy

Meet what I would have well, and it destroy!

Both here and hence pursue me lasting strife,

If, once a widow, ever I be wife!

Ham.

If she should break it now! [To Ophelia.]

Hamlet's talking about Gertrude.

P. King.

'Tis deeply sworn. Sweet, leave me here awhile;

My spirits grow dull, and fain I would beguile

The tedious day with sleep.

[Sleeps.]

P. Queen.

Sleep rock thy brain,

And never come mischance between us twain!

[Exit.]

Ham.

Madam, how like you this play?

Queen.

The lady protests too much, methinks. 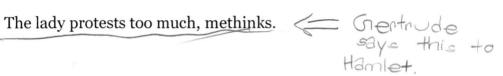 Gertrude says this to Hamlet.

Ham.

O, but she'll keep her word..

King.

Have you heard the argument? Is there no offence in't?

Ham.

No, no! They do but jest, poison in jest; no offence i' the world.

King.

What do you call the play?

Ham.

The Mouse-trap. Marry, how? Tropically. This play is the

image of a murder done in Vienna: Gonzago is the duke's name;

his wife, Baptista: you shall see anon; 'tis a knavish piece of

work: but what o' that? your majesty, and we that have free

souls, it touches us not: let the gall'd jade wince; our withers

are unwrung. ← *Hamlet sees Claudius start to fidget.*

[Enter Lucianus.]

This is one Lucianus, nephew to the King.

Oph.

You are a good chorus, my lord.

Ham.

I could interpret between you and your love, if I could see

the puppets dallying.

Oph.

You are keen, my lord, you are keen.

Ham.

It would cost you a groaning to take off my edge.

Oph.

Still better, and worse.

Ham.

So you must take your husbands. – Begin, murderer; pox, leave

thy damnable faces, and begin. Come: – 'The croaking raven doth

bellow for revenge.'

Luc.

Thoughts black, hands apt, drugs fit, and time agreeing;

Confederate season, else no creature seeing;

Thou mixture rank, of midnight weeds collected,

With Hecate's ban thrice blasted, thrice infected,

Thy natural magic and dire property

On wholesome life usurp immediately.

[Pours the poison into the sleeper's ears.]

Ham.

He poisons him i' the garden for's estate. His name's Gonzago:

The story is extant, and written in very choice Italian; you

shall see anon how the murderer gets the love of Gonzago's wife.

Oph.

The King rises.

Claudius rises and runs from the room.

Ham.

What, frighted with false fire!

Queen.

How fares my lord?

Pol.

Give o'er the play.

King.

Give me some light: — away!

Claudius being exposed on some level.

All.

Lights, lights, lights!

[Exeunt all but Hamlet and Horatio.]

Ham.

Why, let the strucken deer go weep,

The hart ungalled play;

For some must watch, while some must sleep:

So runs the world away. –

Would not this, sir, and a forest of feathers – if the rest of my

fortunes turn Turk with me, – with two Provincial roses on my

razed shoes, get me a fellowship in a cry of players, sir?

Hor.

Half a share.

Ham.

A whole one, I.

For thou dost know, O Damon dear,

This realm dismantled was

Of Jove himself; and now reigns here

A very, very – pajock.

Hor.

You might have rhymed.

Ham.

O good Horatio, I'll take the ghost's word for a thousand
pound! Didst perceive?

Hor.

Very well, my lord.

Ham.

Upon the talk of the poisoning? –

Hor.

I did very well note him.

Ham.

Ah, ha! – Come, some music! Come, the recorders! –

  For if the king like not the comedy,

  Why then, belike he likes it not, perdy.

Come, some music!

[Enter Rosencrantz and Guildenstern.]

Guil.

Good my lord, vouchsafe me a word with you.

Ham.

Sir, a whole history.

Guil.

The king, sir –

Ham.

Ay, sir, what of him?

Guil.

Is, in his retirement, marvellous distempered.

upset / angry

Ham.

With drink, sir?

Guil.

No, my lord; rather with choler.

Ham.

Your wisdom should show itself more richer to signify this to the doctor; for me to put him to his purgation would perhaps plunge him into far more choler.

Guil.

Good my lord, put your discourse into some frame, and start not so wildly from my affair.

Ham.

I am tame, sir: – pronounce.

Guil.

The queen, your mother, in most great affliction of spirit, hath sent me to you. Guildenstern tells Hamlet that his mom wanted to see him?

Ham.

You are welcome.

Guil.

Nay, good my lord, this courtesy is not of the right breed.

If it shall please you to make me a wholesome answer, I will do

your mother's commandment: if not, your pardon and my return

shall be the end of my business.

Ham.

Sir, I cannot.

Guil.

What, my lord?

Ham.

Make you a wholesome answer; my wit's diseased: but, sir, such

Hamlet is being sane again!

answer as I can make, you shall command; or rather, as you say,

my mother: therefore no more, but to the matter: my mother, you

say, —

Ros.

Then thus she says: your behaviour hath struck her into amazement and admiration.

Ham.

O wonderful son, that can so stonish a mother! – But is there no sequel at the heels of this mother's admiration?

Ros.

She desires to speak with you in her closet ere you go to bed.

Ham.

We shall obey, were she ten times our mother. Have you any further trade with us?

Ros.

My lord, you once did love me.

Ham.

And so I do still, by these pickers and stealers.

Ros.

Good my lord, what is your cause of distemper? you do, surely,

bar the door upon your own liberty if you deny your griefs to

your friend.

Ham.

Sir, I lack advancement.

Ros.

How can that be, when you have the voice of the king himself

for your succession in Denmark?

Ham.

Ay, sir, but 'While the grass grows' – the proverb is something

musty.

still around
today!

[Re-enter the Players, with recorders.]

O, the recorders: – let me see one. – To withdraw with you: – why do

you go about to recover the wind of me, as if you would drive me

into a toil?

Guil.

O my lord, if my duty be too bold, my love is too unmannerly.

Ham.

I do not well understand that. Will you play upon this pipe?

Guil.

My lord, I cannot.

Ham.

I pray you.

Guil.

Believe me, I cannot.

Ham.

I do beseech you.

Guil.

I know, no touch of it, my lord.

Ham.

'Tis as easy as lying: govern these ventages with your

finger and thumb, give it breath with your mouth, and it will

discourse most eloquent music. Look you, these are the stops.

Guil.

But these cannot I command to any utterance of harmony; I

have not the skill.

Ham.

Why, look you now, how unworthy a thing you make of me! You

would play upon me; you would seem to know my stops; you would

pluck out the heart of my mystery; you would sound me from my

lowest note to the top of my compass; and there is much music,

excellent voice, in this little organ, yet cannot you make it

speak. 'Sblood, do you think I am easier to be played on than a

pipe? Call me what instrument you will, though you can fret me,

you cannot play upon me.

[Enter Polonius.]

God bless you, sir!

Pol.

My lord, the queen would speak with you, and presently.

Ham.

Do you see yonder cloud that's almost in shape of a camel?

Pol.

By the mass, and 'tis like a camel indeed.

Polonius is just a "yes-man."

Ham.

Methinks it is like a weasel.

Polonius is selfish.

Pol.

It is backed like a weasel.

Ham.

Or like a whale.

Pol.

Very like a whale.

Ham.

Then will I come to my mother by and by. – They fool me to the top of my bent. – I will come by and by.

Pol.

I will say so.

[Exit.]

Ham.

By-and-by is easily said.

[Exit Polonius.]

– Leave me, friends.

[Exeunt Ros, Guil., Hor., and Players.]

Hamlet's 5th soliloquy.

'Tis now the very witching time of night,

When churchyards yawn, and hell itself breathes out

Contagion to this world: now could I drink hot blood,

vengeful,

And do such bitter business as the day

evil

Would quake to look on. Soft! now to my mother. –

O heart, lose not thy nature; let not ever

another illusion

The soul of Nero enter this firm bosom:

Polonius is selfish

Let me be cruel, not unnatural;

I will speak daggers to her, but use none;

He'll get angry @ her w/ words.

Hamlet would like to kill his mom

My tongue and soul in this be hypocrites, –

How in my words somever she be shent,

To give them seals never, my soul, consent!

Q. Who is this person now? how has he changed / different

[Exit.]

Ragefl, murderous, vengeful hot-tempered, re-energized, purposeful, focused;

Scene III. A room in the Castle.

Hamlet is about to finis see his mom!

[Enter King, Rosencrantz, and Guildenstern.]

King. ← Claudius

I like him not; nor stands it safe with us

To let his madness range. Therefore prepare you;

I your commission will forthwith dispatch,

And he to England shall along with you:

The terms of our estate may not endure

Hazard so near us as doth hourly grow

Out of his lunacies.

Hamlet's lunacies Claudius sends Hamlet to England.

Guil.

We will ourselves provide:

Most holy and religious fear it is

To keep those many many bodies safe

That live and feed upon your majesty.

Ros.

The single and peculiar life is bound,

With all the strength and armour of the mind,

To keep itself from 'noyance; but much more

That spirit upon whose weal depend and rest

The lives of many. The cease of majesty

Dies not alone; but like a gulf doth draw

What's near it with it: it is a massy wheel,

Fix'd on the summit of the highest mount,

To whose huge spokes ten thousand lesser things

dominoe effect.

Are mortis'd and adjoin'd; which, when it falls,

Each small annexment, petty consequence,

Attends the boisterous ruin. Never alone

Did the king sigh, but with a general groan.

* The irony is the very person whose loose.

King.

Arm you, I pray you, to this speedy voyage;

For we will fetters put upon this fear,

Which now goes too free-footed.

Ros and Guil.

We will haste us.

[Exeunt Ros. and Guil.]

[Enter Polonius.]

Pol.

My lord, he's going to his mother's closet:

Behind the arras I'll convey myself

To hear the process; I'll warrant she'll tax him home:

And, as you said, and wisely was it said,

'Tis meet that some more audience than a mother,

Since nature makes them partial, should o'erhear

The speech, of vantage. Fare you well, my liege:

I'll call upon you ere you go to bed,

And tell you what I know.

[handwritten: Polonius tells R+G that he's going to ... send Hamlet to England.]

*[handwritten: * Gertrude is Hamlet's mother.]*

King.

Thanks, dear my lord.

[Exit Polonius.]

O, my offence is rank, it smells to heaven;

It hath the primal eldest curse upon't, –

A brother's murder! – Pray can I not,

Though inclination be as sharp as will:

My stronger guilt defeats my strong intent;

And, like a man to double business bound,

I stand in pause where I shall first begin,

And both neglect. What if this cursed hand

Were thicker than itself with brother's blood, –

Is there not rain enough in the sweet heavens

To wash it white as snow? Whereto serves mercy

But to confront the visage of offence?

And what's in prayer but this twofold force, –

To be forestalled ere we come to fall,

Or pardon'd being down? Then I'll look up;

My fault is past. But, O, what form of prayer

Can serve my turn? Forgive me my foul murder! –

That cannot be; since I am still possess'd

Of those effects for which I did the murder, –

My crown, mine own ambition, and my queen.

May one be pardon'd and retain the offence?

In the corrupted currents of this world

Offence's gilded hand may shove by justice;

And oft 'tis seen the wicked prize itself

Buys out the law; but 'tis not so above;

There is no shuffling; – there the action lies

* Rageful, murderous, vengeful, hot-tempered, re-energized, purposeful, focused

In his true nature; and we ourselves compell'd,

Even to the teeth and forehead of our faults,

To give in evidence. What then? what rests?

Try what repentance can: what can it not?

Yet what can it when one cannot repent?

O wretched state! O bosom black as death!

O limed soul, that, struggling to be free,

Art more engag'd! Help, angels! Make assay:

Bow, stubborn knees; and, heart, with strings of steel,

Be soft as sinews of the new-born babe!

All may be well.

[Retires and kneels.]

[Enter Hamlet.]

Ham.

Now might I do it pat, now he is praying;

And now I'll do't; – and so he goes to heaven;

And so am I reveng'd. – that would be scann'd:

A villain kills my father; and for that,

Hamlet's
6th
soliloquy.

I, his sole son, do this same villain send

To heaven.

O, this is hire and salary, not revenge.

He took my father grossly, full of bread;

With all his crimes broad blown, as flush as May;

And how his audit stands, who knows save heaven?

But in our circumstance and course of thought,

'Tis heavy with him: and am I, then, reveng'd,

To take him in the purging of his soul,

When he is fit and season'd for his passage?

No.

Up, sword, and know thou a more horrid hent:

When he is drunk asleep; or in his rage;

Or in the incestuous pleasure of his bed;

At gaming, swearing; or about some act

That has no relish of salvation in't; –

Then trip him, that his heels may kick at heaven;

And that his soul may be as damn'd and black

As hell, whereto it goes. My mother stays:

This physic but prolongs thy sickly days.

[Handwritten margin note, right, top]: Hamlet thinks that Claudius is mourning at the fact that he killed king Hamlet.

[Handwritten margin note, right, bottom]: Hamlet walks by and sees that Claudius is begging on his knees for forgiveness and he wants to kill Claudius

[Handwritten note, bottom]: and wants him to go to the under world

[Exit.]

[The King rises and advances.]

King.

My words fly up, my thoughts remain below:

Words without thoughts never to heaven go.

[Exit.]

whereas if he kills Ha claudius while he's praying, he'll go to heaven. Does he tell everyone what he did? If claudius confesses, he's gotta lose all of his stuff. claudius is wishing for forgiveness. He is not willing to forgive.

Scene IV. Another room in the castle.

[Enter Queen and Polonius.]

Pol.

He will come straight. Look you lay home to him:

Tell him his pranks have been too broad to bear with,

And that your grace hath screen'd and stood between

Much heat and him. I'll silence me e'en here.

Pol. tells Gen. that Ham. is coming

Pray you, be round with him.

Ham.

[Within.] Mother, mother, mother!

Queen.

I'll warrant you:

Fear me not: – withdraw; I hear him coming.

[Polonius goes behind the arras.]

[Enter Hamlet.]

Ham.

Now, mother, what's the matter?

Queen.

Hamlet, thou hast thy father much offended. ← Claudius

Ham.

Mother, you have my father much offended. ← King Hamlet

Queen.

Come, come, you answer with an idle tongue.

Ham.

Go, go, you question with a wicked tongue.

The two

Queen.

Why, how now, Hamlet!

Ham.

What's the matter now?

Queen.

Have you forgot me?

Ham.

No, by the rood, not so:

You are the Queen, your husband's brother's wife,

And, – would it were not so! – you are my mother.

Queen.

Nay, then, I'll set those to you that can speak.

Ham.

Come, come, and sit you down; you shall not budge;

You go not till I set you up a glass

Where you may see the inmost part of you.

Queen.

What wilt thou do? thou wilt not murder me? –

Help, help, ho!

Pol.

[Behind.] What, ho! help, help, help!

Ham.

How now? a rat? [Draws.]

Dead for a ducat, dead!

[Makes a pass through the arras.]

Pol.

[Behind.] O, I am slain!   ← POLONIUS DIES

[Falls and dies.]

Queen.

O me, what hast thou done?

Ham.

Nay, I know not: is it the king?

[Draws forth Polonius.]

Queen.

O, what a rash and bloody deed is this!

Ham.

A bloody deed! – almost as bad, good mother,

As kill a king and marry with his brother.

Queen.

As kill a king!

Ham.

Ay, lady, 'twas my word. –

Thou wretched, rash, intruding fool, farewell!

[To Polonius.] ← Hamlet stabs Pol. thinking its claudius

I took thee for thy better: take thy fortune;

Thou find'st to be too busy is some danger. –

Leave wringing of your hands: peace! sit you down,

And let me wring your heart: for so I shall,

If it be made of penetrable stuff;

If damned custom have not braz'd it so

That it is proof and bulwark against sense.

Queen.

What have I done, that thou dar'st wag thy tongue

In noise so rude against me?

Ham.

Such an act

That blurs the grace and blush of modesty;

Calls virtue hypocrite; takes off the rose

From the fair forehead of an innocent love,

And sets a blister there; makes marriage-vows

As false as dicers' oaths: O, such a deed

As from the body of contraction plucks

The very soul, and sweet religion makes

A rhapsody of words: heaven's face doth glow;

Yea, this solidity and compound mass,

With tristful visage, as against the doom,

Is thought-sick at the act.

Queen.

Ah me, what act,

That roars so loud, and thunders in the index?

she still has no idea what Hamlet is talking about.

Ham.

Look here upon this picture, and on this, –

The counterfeit presentment of two brothers.

See what a grace was seated on this brow;

Hyperion's curls; the front of Jove himself;

An eye like Mars, to threaten and command;

A station like the herald Mercury

New lighted on a heaven-kissing hill:

A combination and a form, indeed,

Where every god did seem to set his seal,

To give the world assurance of a man;

This was your husband. – Look you now what follows:

Here is your husband, like a milldew'd ear

Blasting his wholesome brother. Have you eyes?

she still has no idea what Hamlet's talking about.

Could you on this fair mountain leave to feed,

And batten on this moor? Ha! have you eyes?

You cannot call it love; for at your age

The hey-day in the blood is tame, it's humble,

And waits upon the judgment: and what judgment

Would step from this to this? Sense, sure, you have,

Else could you not have motion: but sure that sense

Is apoplex'd; for madness would not err;

Nor sense to ecstacy was ne'er so thrall'd

But it reserv'd some quantity of choice

To serve in such a difference. What devil was't

That thus hath cozen'd you at hoodman-blind?

Eyes without feeling, feeling without sight,

Ears without hands or eyes, smelling sans all,

Or but a sickly part of one true sense

Could not so mope.

O shame! where is thy blush? Rebellious hell,

If thou canst mutine in a matron's bones,

To flaming youth let virtue be as wax,

And melt in her own fire: proclaim no shame

When the compulsive ardour gives the charge,

Since frost itself as actively doth burn,

And reason panders will.

Queen.

O Hamlet, speak no more:

Thou turn'st mine eyes into my very soul;

And there I see such black and grained spots

As will not leave their tinct.

Ham.

Nay, but to live

In the rank sweat of an enseamed bed,

Stew'd in corruption, honeying and making love

Over the nasty sty, –

Queen.

O, speak to me no more;

These words like daggers enter in mine ears;

No more, sweet Hamlet.

Ham.

A murderer and a villain;

A slave that is not twentieth part the tithe

Of your precedent lord; a vice of kings;

A cutpurse of the empire and the rule,

That from a shelf the precious diadem stole

And put it in his pocket!

Hamlet puts his mother down

Queen.

No more.

Ham.

A king of shreds and patches! –

[Enter Ghost.]

Save me and hover o'er me with your wings,

You heavenly guards! – What would your gracious figure?

Queen.

Alas, he's mad!

The ghost has entered. The queen cannot see or hear him.

Ham.

Do you not come your tardy son to chide,

That, laps'd in time and passion, lets go by

The important acting of your dread command?

O, say!

Ghost.

Do not forget. This visitation

Is but to whet thy almost blunted purpose.

But, look, amazement on thy mother sits:

O, step between her and her fighting soul, –

Conceit in weakest bodies strongest works, –

Speak to her, Hamlet.

King Hamlet reminds Hamlet to not forget the unwanted purpose.

Ham.

How is it with you, lady?

Queen.

Alas, how is't with you,

That you do bend your eye on vacancy,

And with the incorporal air do hold discourse?

Forth at your eyes your spirits wildly peep;

And, as the sleeping soldiers in the alarm,

Your bedded hairs, like life in excrements,

Start up and stand an end. O gentle son,

Upon the heat and flame of thy distemper

Sprinkle cool patience! Whereon do you look?

Ham.

On him, on him! Look you how pale he glares!

His form and cause conjoin'd, preaching to stones,

Would make them capable. – Do not look upon me;

Lest with this piteous action you convert

My stern effects: then what I have to do

Will want true colour; tears perchance for blood.

Queen.

To whom do you speak this?

Ham.

Do you see nothing there?

Queen.

Nothing at all; yet all that is I see.

Ham.

Nor did you nothing hear?

Queen.

No, nothing but ourselves.

Ham.

Why, look you there! look how it steals away!

My father, in his habit as he liv'd!

Look, where he goes, even now out at the portal!

203 | P a g e

Hamlet talks about the ghost of his father whose leaving the room.

[Exit Ghost.]

Queen.

This is the very coinage of your brain:

This bodiless creation ecstasy

Is very cunning in.

Gertrude thinks Hamlet has gone nuts once he saw his father's ghost.

Ham.

Ecstasy! ←——— *diseased words*

My pulse, as yours, doth temperately keep time,

And makes as healthful music: it is not madness

That I have utter'd: bring me to the test,

And I the matter will re-word; which madness

Would gambol from. Mother, for love of grace,

Hamlet is mad at his mom because she married Claudius.

Lay not that flattering unction to your soul

That not your trespass, but my madness speaks:

It will but skin and film the ulcerous place,

Whilst rank corruption, mining all within,

Infects unseen. Confess yourself to heaven;

Repent what's past; avoid what is to come;

And do not spread the compost on the weeds,

To make them ranker. Forgive me this my virtue;

For in the fatness of these pursy times

Virtue itself of vice must pardon beg,

Yea, curb and woo for leave to do him good.

Queen.

O Hamlet, thou hast cleft my heart in twain.  *diseased phrase*

Ham.

O, throw away the worser part of it,

And live the purer with the other half.

Good night: but go not to mine uncle's bed;

Assume a virtue, if you have it not.

That monster custom, who all sense doth eat,

Of habits evil, is angel yet in this, –

That to the use of actions fair and good

He likewise gives a frock or livery

That aptly is put on. Refrain to-night;

And that shall lend a kind of easiness

To the next abstinence: the next more easy;

For use almost can change the stamp of nature,

And either curb the devil, or throw him out

With wondrous potency. Once more, good-night:

And when you are desirous to be bles'd,

I'll blessing beg of you. – For this same lord

[Pointing to Polonius.]

I do repent; but heaven hath pleas'd it so,

To punish me with this, and this with me,

That I must be their scourge and minister.

I will bestow him, and will answer well

The death I gave him. So again, good-night. –

I must be cruel, only to be kind:

Thus bad begins, and worse remains behind. –

One word more, good lady.

Queen.

What shall I do?

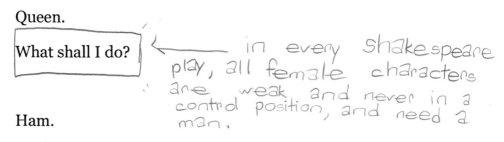

in every shakespeare play, all female characters are weak and never in a control position, and need a man.

Ham.

Not this, by no means, that I bid you do:

Let the bloat king tempt you again to bed;

Pinch wanton on your cheek; call you his mouse;

And let him, for a pair of reechy kisses,

Or paddling in your neck with his damn'd fingers,

Make you to ravel all this matter out,

That I essentially am not in madness,

But mad in craft. 'Twere good you let him know;

For who that's but a queen, fair, sober, wise,

Would from a paddock, from a bat, a gib,

Such dear concernings hide? who would do so?

No, in despite of sense and secrecy,

Unpeg the basket on the house's top,

Let the birds fly, and, like the famous ape,

To try conclusions, in the basket creep

And break your own neck down.

Hamlet tells Gertrude to not spend the night with claudius.

Queen.

Be thou assur'd, if words be made of breath,

And breath of life, I have no life to breathe

What thou hast said to me.

Ham.

I must to England; you know that?

Queen.

Alack,

I had forgot: 'tis so concluded on.

Ham.

There's letters seal'd: and my two schoolfellows, –

Whom I will trust as I will adders fang'd, –

They bear the mandate; they must sweep my way

And marshal me to knavery. Let it work;

For 'tis the sport to have the enginer

Hoist with his own petard: and 't shall go hard

But I will delve one yard below their mines

And blow them at the moon: O, 'tis most sweet,

When in one line two crafts directly meet. –

This man shall set me packing:

I'll lug the guts into the neighbour room. –

Mother, good-night. – Indeed, this counsellor

Is now most still, most secret, and most grave,

Who was in life a foolish peating knave.

Come, sir, to draw toward an end with you: –

Good night, mother.

[Exeunt severally; Hamlet, dragging out Polonius.]

ACT IV.

Scene I. A room in the Castle.

[Enter King, Queen, Rosencrantz and Guildenstern.]

King.

There's matter in these sighs. These profound heaves

You must translate: 'tis fit we understand them.

Where is your son?

Queen.

Bestow this place on us a little while.

[To Rosencrantz and Guildenstern, who go out.]

Gertrude either spills the beans or is she going to be cool.

Ah, my good lord, what have I seen to-night!

King.

What, Gertrude? How does Hamlet?

Queen.

Keeping promise to Hamlet

Mad as the sea and wind, when both contend ⟵ *keeping promise to Hamlet.*

Which is the mightier: in his lawless fit

Behind the arras hearing something stir,

Whips out his rapier, cries 'A rat, a rat!' *There's no hiding Polonius.*

And in this brainish apprehension, kills *Claudius*

The unseen good old man. ⟵ *Polonius*

King.

O heavy deed!

It had been so with us, had we been there:

Hamlet is a threat to everyone

His liberty is full of threats to all; *setting to ship off Hamlet.*

To you yourself, to us, to every one. *setting up to ship off Hamlet*

Alas, how shall this bloody deed be answer'd?— *what are we gonna do?*

what are we gonna do?

It will be laid to us, whose providence

Should have kept short, restrain'd, and out of haunt

This mad young man. But so much was our love *How are we going to explain this.*

We would not understand what was most fit;

But, like the owner of a foul disease,

To keep it from divulging, let it feed

Even on the pith of life. Where is he gone?

Queen.

To draw apart the body he hath kill'd:

O'er whom his very madness, like some ore

Among a mineral of metals base,

Shows itself pure: he weeps for what is done.

Hamlet took Polonius's body out.

King.

O Gertrude, come away!

Claudius

The sun no sooner shall the mountains touch

But we will ship him hence: and this vile deed

We must with all our majesty and skill

Both countenance and excuse. – Ho, Guildenstern!

[Re-enter Rosencrantz and Guildenstern.]

Friends both, go join you with some further aid:

Hamlet in madness hath Polonius slain,

And from his mother's closet hath he dragg'd him:

Go seek him out; speak fair, and bring the body

Into the chapel. I pray you, haste in this.

[Exeunt Rosencrantz and Guildenstern.]

Come, Gertrude, we'll call up our wisest friends;

And let them know both what we mean to do

And what's untimely done: so haply slander, –

Whose whisper o'er the world's diameter,

As level as the cannon to his blank,

Transports his poison'd shot, – may miss our name,

And hit the woundless air. – O, come away!

My soul is full of discord and dismay.

Claudius is two-faced and infront of Gertrude he lies all the time. we know that he is worried about himself.

different person in front of gertude, he thinks she doesnt know anything

[Exeunt.]

Scene II. Another room in the Castle.

[Enter Hamlet.]

Ham.

Safely stowed.

Ros. and Guil.

[Within.] Hamlet! Lord Hamlet!

Ham.

What noise? who calls on Hamlet? O, here they come.

[Enter Rosencrantz and Guildenstern.] ← R + G + Ger. are the only ones who know that Polonius is dead.

Ros.

What have you done, my lord, with the dead body? (Hamlet killed him thinking that it was Claudius hiding behind the tapestry.)

Polonius

Gertrude

Ham.

Compounded it with dust, whereto 'tis kin.

Ros.

Tell us where 'tis, that we may take it thence,

And bear it to the chapel.

Ham.

Do not believe it.

Ros.

Believe what?

Ham.

That I can keep your counsel, and not mine own. Besides, to be

demanded of a sponge! – what replication should be made by the son

of a king?

Ros.

Take you me for a sponge, my lord? ← *Hamlet thinks that Rosencrantz is just plain dumb.*

Ham.

Ay, sir; that soaks up the King's countenance, his rewards,

his authorities. But such officers do the king best service in

the end: he keeps them, like an ape, in the corner of his jaw;

first mouthed, to be last swallowed: when he needs what you have

gleaned, it is but squeezing you, and, sponge, you shall be dry

again.

Ros.

I understand you not, my lord.

Ham.

I am glad of it: a knavish speech sleeps in a foolish ear.

Ros.

My lord, you must tell us where the body is and go with us to the king.

Ham.

The body is with the king, but the king is not with the body.

The king is a thing, – ← —— Hamlet "says" that Polonius's body is with the king.

Guil.

A thing, my lord!

Ham.

Of nothing: bring me to him. Hide fox, and all after.

[Exeunt.]

Scene III. Another room in the Castle.

[Enter King,attended.]

King.

I have sent to seek him and to find the body.

How dangerous is it that this man goes loose! *ironic* ← *ironic:*

it is ironic because

Yet must not we put the strong law on him:

He's lov'd of the distracted multitude,

Who like not in their judgment, but their eyes;

And where 'tis so, the offender's scourge is weigh'd,

But never the offence. To bear all smooth and even,

This sudden sending him away must seem

Deliberate pause: diseases desperate grown

By desperate appliance are reliev'd,

Or not at all.

[Enter Rosencrantz.]

How now! what hath befall'n?

Ros.

Where the dead body is bestow'd, my lord,

We cannot get from him.

King.

But where is he?

Handwritten note: ✳ Hamlet is not willing to reveal where he hid Polonius's body.

Ros.

Without, my lord; guarded, to know your pleasure.

King.

Bring him before us.

Ros.

Ho, Guildenstern! bring in my lord.

[Enter Hamlet and Guildenstern.]

King.

Now, Hamlet, where's Polonius?

Ham.

At supper.

King.

At supper! where? ← *He is decomposing Life ends up being nothing once we all are there.*

Ham.

cycle of life

Not where he eats, but where he is eaten: a certain

convocation of politic worms are e'en at him. Your worm is your
Cycle of life Hamlet lies to Clau- dius.

only emperor for diet: we fat all creatures else to fat us, and

we fat ourselves for maggots: your fat king and your lean beggar

is but variable service, – two dishes, but to one table: that's
people *grave*

the end.

He says that this is basically life.

King.

Alas, alas!

Ham.

A man may fish with the worm that hath eat of a king, and eat of the fish that hath fed of that worm. ← *metaphor*

King.

What dost thou mean by this?

Ham.

Nothing but to show you how a king may go a progress through

the guts of a beggar.

King.

Where is Polonius?

Ham.

In heaven: send thither to see: if your messenger find him not

there, seek him i' the other place yourself. But, indeed, if you

find him not within this month, you shall nose him as you go up
Hell

the stairs into the lobby.

He alludes to the place to where he could be. Polonius is on the stairs somewhere.

King.

Go seek him there. [To some Attendants.]

Ham.

He will stay till you come.

[Exeunt Attendants.]

King.

Hamlet, this deed, for thine especial safety, –

Which we do tender, as we dearly grieve

For that which thou hast done, – must send thee hence

With fiery quickness: therefore prepare thyself;

The bark is ready, and the wind at help,

The associates tend, and everything is bent

For England.

Claudius tells Hamlet that he's going to England.

Ham.

For England!

King.

Ay, Hamlet.

Ham.

Good.

claudius plans to kill Hamlet ←← ←

King.

So is it, if thou knew'st our purposes.

Ham.

I see a cherub that sees them. – But, come; for England! –

Farewell, dear mother. ←← *Hamlet has no clue why he is being sent to England, but he eventually figures out why.*

King.

Thy loving father, Hamlet.

Ham.

My mother: father and mother is man and wife; man and wife is

one flesh; and so, my mother. – Come, for England!

[Exit.]

King.

Follow him at foot; tempt him with speed aboard;

Delay it not; I'll have him hence to-night:

Away! for everything is seal'd and done

That else leans on the affair: pray you, make haste.

[Exeunt Rosencrantz and Guildenstern.]

And, England, if my love thou hold'st at aught, –

As my great power thereof may give thee sense,

Since yet thy cicatrice looks raw and red

After the Danish sword, and thy free awe

Pays homage to us, – thou mayst not coldly set

Our sovereign process; which imports at full,

By letters conjuring to that effect,

The present death of Hamlet. Do it, England;

For like the hectic in my blood he rages,

And thou must cure me: till I know 'tis done,

Howe'er my haps, my joys were ne'er begun.

[Exit.]

Handwritten margin notes: Claudius decides to kill Hamlet.... He plans to send him to England where he is going to be sentenced to death. There is a hub of

Handwritten note at bottom: He is going to write a letter to the king of England to kill Hamlet.

Scene IV. A plain in Denmark. ← LOCATION

[Enter Fortinbras, and Forces marching.]

Hamlet somehow escapes from England

For.

Go, Captain, from me greet the Danish king:

7th soliloquy is in the play.

Tell him that, by his license, Fortinbras

Craves the conveyance of a promis'd march

Over his kingdom. You know the rendezvous.

If that his majesty would aught with us,

Both king Ham. + king

We shall express our duty in his eye;

And let him know so.

For. fathers have died.

Capt. ← *Captain of boat.*

I will do't, my lord.

Both are going and through the same thing.

living

For.

Go softly on.

[Exeunt all For. and Forces.]

[Enter Hamlet, Rosencrantz, Guildenstern, &c.]

Ham.

Good sir, whose powers are these?

Capt.

They are of Norway, sir.

Fortinbras was there for one reason which he

Ham.

How purpos'd, sir, I pray you?

Capt.

Against some part of Poland.

Ham.

Who commands them, sir?

Capt.

The nephew to old Norway, Fortinbras.

Ham.

Goes it against the main of Poland, sir,

Or for some frontier?

Capt.

Truly to speak, and with no addition,

We go to gain a little patch of ground

That hath in it no profit but the name.

To pay five ducats, five, I would not farm it;

Nor will it yield to Norway or the Pole

A ranker rate, should it be sold in fee.

Ham.

Why, then the Polack never will defend it.

Capt.

Yes, it is already garrison'd.

Ham.

Two thousand souls and twenty thousand ducats

Will not debate the question of this straw:

This is the imposthume of much wealth and peace,

That inward breaks, and shows no cause without

Why the man dies. – I humbly thank you, sir.

Capt.

God b' wi' you, sir.

[Exit.]

Ros.

Will't please you go, my lord?

Ham.

I'll be with you straight. Go a little before.

[Exeunt all but Hamlet.]

HAMLET'S 7th SILILOQUY

How all occasions do inform against me

And spur my dull revenge! What is a man,

If his chief good and market of his time

Be but to sleep and feed? a beast, no more.

Sure he that made us with such large discourse,

Looking before and after, gave us not

That capability and godlike reason

To fust in us unus'd. Now, whether it be

Bestial oblivion, or some craven scruple

Of thinking too precisely on the event, –

A thought which, quarter'd, hath but one part wisdom

And ever three parts coward, – I do not know

Why yet I live to say 'This thing's to do;'

Sith I have cause, and will, and strength, and means

To do't. Examples, gross as earth, exhort me:

Witness this army, of such mass and charge,

Led by a delicate and tender prince;

Whose spirit, with divine ambition puff'd,

Makes mouths at the invisible event;

Exposing what is mortal and unsure

To all that fortune, death, and danger dare,

Even for an egg-shell. Rightly to be great

Is not to stir without great argument,

But greatly to find quarrel in a straw

When honour's at the stake. How stand I, then,

That have a father kill'd, a mother stain'd,

Excitements of my reason and my blood,

And let all sleep? while, to my shame, I see

The imminent death of twenty thousand men

That, for a fantasy and trick of fame,

Go to their graves like beds; fight for a plot

Whereon the numbers cannot try the cause,

Which is not tomb enough and continent

To hide the slain? – O, from thi   forth,

My thoughts be bloody, or be   g worth!

[Exit.]

Scene V. Elsinore. A room in the Castle.

[Enter Queen and Horatio.]

Queen.

I will not speak with her.

Gent.

She is importunate; indeed distract:

Her mood will needs be pitied.

Queen.

What would she have?

Gent. ⟵—— Horatio?

She speaks much of her father; says she hears

There's tricks i' the world, and hems, and beats her heart;

Spurns enviously at straws; speaks things in doubt,

That carry but half sense: her speech is nothing,

Yet the unshaped use of it doth move

The hearers to collection; they aim at it,

And botch the words up fit to their own thoughts;

Which, as her winks, and nods, and gestures yield them,

Indeed would make one think there might be thought,

Though nothing sure, yet much unhappily.

'Twere good she were spoken with; for she may strew

Dangerous conjectures in ill-breeding minds.

Horatio tells the queen
that Ophelia is mourning
over her father's death!

Queen.

✳ Horatio

Let her come in.

[Exit Horatio.]

To my sick soul, as sin's true nature is,

Each toy seems Prologue to some great amiss:

So full of artless jealousy is guilt,

It spills itself in fearing to be spilt.

[Re-enter Horatio with Ophelia.]

Oph.

Where is the beauteous majesty of Denmark?

Queen.

How now, Ophelia?

Oph. [Sings.]

How should I your true love know

From another one?

By his cockle bat and' staff

And his sandal shoon.

Queen.

Alas, sweet lady, what imports this song?

Oph. *WHO IS SHE SAYING IT TO???*

Say you? nay, pray you, mark.

[Sings.]

He is dead and gone, lady,

He is dead and gone;

At his head a grass green turf,

At his heels a stone.

Ophelia finds out that her father has died. Hint: Ophelia will kill herself by drowning in a river due to her father's death.

Queen.

Nay, but Ophelia –

Oph.

Pray you, mark.

[Sings.]

White his shroud as the mountain snow,

[Enter King.]

Queen.

Alas, look here, my lord!

Claudius ~~pla~~ comes in and hopes that someone can help the poor Ophelia!

Oph.

[Sings.]

> Larded all with sweet flowers;
>
> Which bewept to the grave did go
>
> With true-love showers.

who is she singing the song to?

King.

How do you, pretty lady?

Oph.

Well, God dild you! They say the owl was a baker's daughter.

Lord, we know what we are, but know not what we may be. God be at

your table!

King.

Conceit upon her father.

Oph.

Pray you, let's have no words of this; but when they ask you what

it means, say you this:

[Sings.]

   To-morrow is Saint Valentine's day

    All in the morning bedtime,

   And I a maid at your window,

    To be your Valentine.

Ophelia's famous song!

   Then up he rose and donn'd his clothes,

    And dupp'd the chamber door,

   Let in the maid, that out a maid

    Never departed more.

King.

Pretty Ophelia!

Oph.

Indeed, la, without an oath, I'll make an end on't:

[Sings.]

  By Gis and by Saint Charity,

    Alack, and fie for shame!

  Young men will do't if they come to't;

    By cock, they are to blame.

  Quoth she, before you tumbled me,

    You promis'd me to wed.

  So would I ha' done, by yonder sun,

    An thou hadst not come to my bed.

King.

How long hath she been thus?

Oph.

I hope all will be well. We must be patient: but I cannot

choose but weep, to think they would lay him i' the cold ground.

My brother shall know of it: and so I thank you for your good

counsel. – Come, my coach! – Good night, ladies; good night, sweet

ladies; good night, good night.

LAERTES KNOWS
[Exit.] ABOUT POLONIUS's DEATH!

King.

Follow her close; give her good watch, I pray you.

[Exit Horatio.]

O, this is the poison of deep grief; it springs

All from her father's death. O Gertrude, Gertrude, DOUBLE

When sorrows come, they come not single spies, MEANI NG:

But in battalions! First, her father slain:

Next, your son gone; and he most violent author

Of his own just remove: the people muddied, Literally: Hamlet is gone

Thick and and unwholesome in their thoughts and whispers Figuratively: Her father

For good Polonius' death; and we have done but greenly is dead.

In hugger-mugger to inter him: poor Ophelia

Divided from herself and her fair judgment,

Without the which we are pictures or mere beasts:

Last, and as much containing as all these,

Her brother is in secret come from France;

Feeds on his wonder, keeps himself in clouds,

And wants not buzzers to infect his ear

With pestilent speeches of his father's death;

Wherein necessity, of matter beggar'd,

Will nothing stick our person to arraign

In ear and ear. O my dear Gertrude, this,

Like to a murdering piece, in many places

Give, me superfluous death.

[A noise within.]

Queen.

Alack, what noise is this?

King.

Where are my Switzers? let them guard the door.

[Enter a Gentleman.]

What is the matter?

Gent.

Save yourself, my lord:

The ocean, overpeering of his list,

Eats not the flats with more impetuous haste

Than young Laertes, in a riotous head,

O'erbears your offices. The rabble call him lord;

And, as the world were now but to begin,

Antiquity forgot, custom not known,

The ratifiers and props of every word,

They cry 'Choose we! Laertes shall be king!'

Caps, hands, and tongues applaud it to the clouds,

'Laertes shall be king! Laertes king!'

Queen.

How cheerfully on the false trail they cry!

O, this is counter, you false Danish dogs!

[A noise within.]

King.

The doors are broke.

[Enter Laertes, armed; Danes following.]

Laer.

Where is this king? – Sirs, stand you all without.

Danes.

No, let's come in.

Laer.

I pray you, give me leave.

Danes.

We will, we will.

[They retire without the door.]

Laer.

I thank you: – keep the door. – O thou vile king,

Give me my father!

Queen.

Calmly, good Laertes.

Laer.

That drop of blood that's calm proclaims me bastard;

Cries cuckold to my father; brands the harlot

Even here, between the chaste unsmirched brow

Of my true mother. ←——— Laertes is mad!!!

King.

What is the cause, Laertes,

That thy rebellion looks so giant-like? –

Let him go, Gertrude; do not fear our person:

There's such divinity doth hedge a king,

That treason can but peep to what it would,

Acts little of his will. – Tell me, Laertes,

Why thou art thus incens'd. – Let him go, Gertrude: –

Speak, man.

Laer.

Where is my father?

King.

Dead.

Queen.

But not by him.

she knows that he is dead. why does she do that?

King.

Let him demand his fill.

Laer.

How came he dead? I'll not be juggled with:

To hell, allegiance! vows, to the blackest devil!

Conscience and grace, to the profoundest pit!

I dare damnation: – to this point I stand, –

That both the worlds, I give to negligence,

Let come what comes; only I'll be reveng'd

Most throughly for my father.

LAERTES GOES ON A RAGE

Laertes wants to revenge for his father's death

King.

Who shall stay you?

Laer. Ham. For.

RE
VENGE

Laer.

My will, not all the world:

And for my means, I'll husband them so well,

They shall go far with little.

King.

Good Laertes,

If you desire to know the certainty

Of your dear father's death, is't writ in your revenge

That, sweepstake, you will draw both friend and foe,

Winner and loser?

Laer.

None but his enemies.

King.

Will you know them then?

Laer.

To his good friends thus wide I'll ope my arms;

And, like the kind life-rendering pelican,

Repast them with my blood.

King.

Why, now you speak

Like a good child and a true gentleman.

That I am guiltless of your father's death, ← *He is not. He was in on the whole thing! Claudius is manipulating ~~eta~~ Laertes*

And am most sensibly in grief for it,

It shall as level to your judgment pierce

As day does to your eye.

Danes.

[Within] Let her come in.

Laer.

How now! What noise is that?

[Re-enter Ophelia, fantastically dressed with straws and flowers.]

O heat, dry up my brains! tears seven times salt,

Burn out the sense and virtue of mine eye! –

By heaven, thy madness shall be paid by weight,

Till our scale turn the beam. O rose of May!

Dear maid, kind sister, sweet Ophelia! –

O heavens! is't possible a young maid's wits

Should be as mortal as an old man's life?

Nature is fine in love; and where 'tis fine,

It sends some precious instance of itself

After the thing it loves.

Oph.

[Sings.]

   They bore him barefac'd on the bier

   Hey no nonny, nonny, hey nonny

   And on his grave rain'd many a tear. –

Fare you well, my dove!

Laer.

Hadst thou thy wits, and didst persuade revenge,

It could not move thus.

Oph.

You must sing 'Down a-down, an you call him a-down-a.' O,

how the wheel becomes it! It is the false steward, that stole his

master's daughter.

Laer.

This nothing's more than matter.

Oph.

There's rosemary, that's for remembrance; pray, love,

remember: and there is pansies, that's for thoughts.

Laer.

A document in madness, – thoughts and remembrance fitted.

Oph.

There's fennel for you, and columbines: – there's rue for you;

and here's some for me: – we may call it herb of grace o'

Sundays: – O, you must wear your rue with a difference. – There's a

daisy: – I would give you some violets, but they wither'd all when my father died: – they say he made a good end, –

[Sings.]

  For bonny sweet Robin is all my joy, –

Laer.

Thought and affliction, passion, hell itself,

She turns to favour and to prettiness.

Oph.

[Sings.]

  And will he not come again?

  And will he not come again?

    No, no, he is dead,

    Go to thy death-bed,

  He never will come again.

  His beard was as white as snow,

  All flaxen was his poll:

    He is gone, he is gone,

    And we cast away moan:

  God ha' mercy on his soul!

And of all Christian souls, I pray God. – God b' wi' ye.

[Exit.]

Laer.

Do you see this, O God?

King.

Laertes, I must commune with your grief,

Or you deny me right. Go but apart,

Make choice of whom your wisest friends you will,

And they shall hear and judge 'twixt you and me.

If by direct or by collateral hand

They find us touch'd, we will our kingdom give,

Our crown, our life, and all that we call ours,

To you in satisfaction; but if not,

Be you content to lend your patience to us,

And we shall jointly labour with your soul

To give it due content.

Laer.

Let this be so;

His means of death, his obscure burial, –

No trophy, sword, nor hatchment o'er his bones,

No noble rite nor formal ostentation, –

Cry to be heard, as 'twere from heaven to earth,

That I must call't in question.

No proper ceromony happened. Claudius goes and talks to Laertes.

King.

So you shall;

And where the offence is let the great axe fall.

I pray you go with me.

[Exeunt.]

DUAL MEANING
FIGURATIVELY: Justice (be on my side)
Literally: I have an act planned (come with me)

Scene VI. Another room in the Castle.

[Enter Horatio and a Servant.]

Hor.

What are they that would speak with me?

Servant.

Sailors, sir: they say they have letters for you.

Hor.

Let them come in.

[Exit Servant.]

I do not know from what part of the world

I should be greeted, if not from Lord Hamlet.

[Enter Sailors.]

I Sailor.

☆ it is not a big thing. (hint hint: next scene scene 7)

If Laertes got back for a few days, Hamlet has already left to England.

God bless you, sir.

Hor.

Let him bless thee too.

Sailor.

He shall, sir, an't please him. There's a letter for you,

sir, – it comes from the ambassador that was bound for England; if

your name be Horatio, as I am let to know it is.

Letter from Hamlet

Hor.

[Reads.] 'Horatio, when thou shalt have overlooked

this, give these fellows some means to the king: they have

letters for him. Ere we were two days old at sea, a pirate of

very warlike appointment gave us chase. Finding ourselves too

slow of sail, we put on a compelled valour, and in the grapple I

boarded them: on the instant they got clear of our ship; so I

alone became their prisoner. They have dealt with me like thieves

of mercy: but they knew what they did; I am to do a good turn for

them. Let the king have the letters I have sent; and repair thou

to me with as much haste as thou wouldst fly death. I have words

Hamlet's letter to Claudius

to speak in thine ear will make thee dumb; yet are they much too

light for the bore of the matter. These good fellows will bring

thee where I am. Rosencrantz and Guildenstern hold their course

for England: of them I have much to tell thee. Farewell.

He that thou knowest thine,   HAMLET.'

[Handwritten note: Claudius has a letter from Hamlet. He got imprisoned by pirates and treated him good. R+G are still going to England? why?]

Come, I will give you way for these your letters;

And do't the speedier, that you may direct me

To him from whom you brought them.

[Handwritten note: Horatio goes to talk to Hamlet.]

[Exeunt.]

[Handwritten note: IRONY that occurs! without this scene the end of the play would not have happened.]

Scene VII. Another room in the Castle.

[Enter King and Laertes.]

King.

Now must your conscience my acquittance seal,

And you must put me in your heart for friend,

Sith you have heard, and with a knowing ear,

That he which hath your noble father slain ← Polonius died.

Pursu'd my life.

Laer.

It well appears: – but tell me

Why you proceeded not against these feats,

So crimeful and so capital in nature,

As by your safety, wisdom, all things else,

You mainly were stirr'd up.

Laertes wants justice

King. ← Claudius

O, for two special reasons;

Which may to you, perhaps, seem much unsinew'd,

But yet to me they are strong. The queen his mother

Lives almost by his looks; and for myself, –

My virtue or my plague, be it either which, –

The two reasons that Hamlet can't be killed?

She's so conjunctive to my life and soul,

That, as the star moves not but in his sphere,

I could not but by her. The other motive,

Why to a public count I might not go,

Is the great love the general gender bear him;

Who, dipping all his faults in their affection,

Would, like the spring that turneth wood to stone,

Convert his gyves to graces; so that my arrows,

SECOND REASON

Too slightly timber'd for so loud a wind,

Would have reverted to my bow again,

And not where I had aim'd them.

Laer.

And so have I a noble father lost; ← *He is saying that he lost his father.*

A sister driven into desperate terms, –

Whose worth, if praises may go back again, *He wants jus*

Stood challenger on mount of all the age

For her perfections: – but my revenge will come. ← *Hint: Laertes eventually avenges his father's death. His revenge will come.*

King.

Break not your sleeps for that: – you must not think

That we are made of stuff so flat and dull

That we can let our beard be shook with danger,

And think it pastime. You shortly shall hear more:

I lov'd your father, and we love ourself; ← *ironic:*

ironic???

imagine that he already took care of the prob.

And that, I hope, will teach you to imagine, –

[Enter a Messenger.]

How now! What news?

Mess.

Letters, my lord, from Hamlet:

This to your majesty; this to the queen.

[handwritten: Hamlet has written letters to both the queen and king.]

King.

From Hamlet! Who brought them?

[handwritten: The messenger brought claudius the letters from Hamlet.]

Mess.

Sailors, my lord, they say; I saw them not:

They were given me by Claudio: – he receiv'd them

Of him that brought them.

King.

Laertes, you shall hear them.

Leave us.

[Exit Messenger.]

[Reads]'High and mighty, – You shall know I am set naked on your kingdom. To-morrow shall I beg leave to see your kingly eyes: when I shall, first asking your pardon thereunto, recount the occasions of my sudden and more strange return.   HAMLET.'

What should this mean? Are all the rest come back?

Or is it some abuse, and no such thing?

Laer.

Know you the hand?

Hint Hint: Claudius thinks of another plan to kill Hamlet

King.

'Tis Hamlet's character: – 'Naked!' –

And in a postscript here, he says 'alone.'

Can you advise me?

Laer.

I am lost in it, my lord. But let him come;

It warms the very sickness in my heart

That I shall live and tell him to his teeth,

'Thus didest thou.'

King.

If it be so, Laertes, –

As how should it be so? how otherwise? –

Will you be rul'd by me?

Laer.

Ay, my lord;

So you will not o'errule me to a peace.

King.

To thine own peace. If he be now return'd –

As checking at his voyage, and that he means

No more to undertake it, – I will work him

To exploit, now ripe in my device,

Under the which he shall not choose but fall:

And for his death no wind shall breathe;

But even his mother shall uncharge the practice

going to set a trap up to kill Hamlet and make it look like an accident

And call it accident.

Laer.

My lord, I will be rul'd;

The rather if you could devise it so

That I might be the organ.

Hint Hint:
Hamlet and Laertes
have a sword match
in order for Laertes
to avenge his
father's
death.
asking if he may kill
Hamlet

King.

It falls right. ⟵――――

You have been talk'd of since your travel much,

And that in Hamlet's hearing, for a quality

Wherein they say you shine: your sum of parts

Did not together pluck such envy from him

As did that one; and that, in my regard,

Of the unworthiest siege.

Claudius
runs with
the plan.
"flattering"

Laer.

What part is that, my lord?

King.

A very riband in the cap of youth,

Yet needful too; for youth no less becomes

The light and careless livery that it wears

Than settled age his sables and his weeds,

Importing health and graveness. – Two months since,

Here was a gentleman of Normandy, –

I've seen myself, and serv'd against, the French,

And they can well on horseback: but this gallant

Had witchcraft in't: he grew unto his seat;

And to such wondrous doing brought his horse,

As had he been incorps'd and demi-natur'd

With the brave beast: so far he topp'd my thought

That I, in forgery of shapes and tricks,

Come short of what he did.

some guy made up stories about Laertes being good with the sword.

Laer.

A Norman was't? ←

King.

A Norman.

Laer.

Upon my life, Lamond.

King.

The very same.

Laer.

I know him well: he is the brooch indeed

And gem of all the nation.

King.

He made confession of you;

And gave you such a masterly report

For art and exercise in your defence,

And for your rapier most especially,

That he cried out, 'twould be a sight indeed

If one could match you: the scrimers of their nation

He swore, had neither motion, guard, nor eye,

If you oppos'd them. Sir, this report of his

Did Hamlet so envenom with his envy

That he could nothing do but wish and beg

Your sudden coming o'er, to play with him.

Now, out of this, –

Laer.

What out of this, my lord?

King.

Laertes, was your father dear to you?

Or are you like the painting of a sorrow,

A face without a heart?

Laer.

Why ask you this?

King.

Not that I think you did not love your father;

But that I know love is begun by time,

claudius lies ???

And that I see, in passages of proof,

Time qualifies the spark and fire of it.

There lives within the very flame of love

A kind of wick or snuff that will abate it;

And nothing is at a like goodness still;

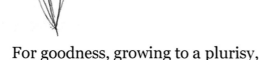

For goodness, growing to a plurisy,

Dies in his own too much: that we would do,

We should do when we would; for this 'would' changes,

And hath abatements and delays as many

As there are tongues, are hands, are accidents;

And then this 'should' is like a spendthrift sigh,

That hurts by easing. But to the quick o' the ulcer: –

Hamlet comes back: what would you undertake

To show yourself your father's son in deed

More than in words?

Talking about how to treat Hamlet when he gets back.

Laer.

To cut his throat i' the church.

Laertes plans on cutting Hamlet's throat

"flattering about how good he is at fencing!!

How Laertes plans to kill Hamlet.

King.

No place, indeed, should murder sanctuarize;

Revenge should have no bounds. But, good Laertes,

Will you do this, keep close within your chamber.

Hamlet return'd shall know you are come home:

We'll put on those shall praise your excellence

And set a double varnish on the fame

The Frenchman gave you; bring you in fine together

And wager on your heads: he, being remiss,

Most generous, and free from all contriving,

Will not peruse the foils; so that with ease,

Or with a little shuffling, you may choose

A sword unbated, and, in a pass of practice, ← *really sharp sword!*

1st plan: poison sword.

really sharp
Requite him for your father.

2nd plan: poison his drink

Laer.

I will do't:

And for that purpose I'll anoint my sword

Laertes poison his sword poisoned his sword

I bought an unction of a mountebank,

So mortal that, but dip a knife in it,

NO cure
Where it draws blood no cataplasm so rare, *no medicine can help*

Collected from all simples that have virtue

Under the moon, can save the thing from death

This is but scratch'd withal: I'll touch my point

With this contagion, that, if I gall him slightly,

It may be death. ← *it could lead to his death.*

King.

Let's further think of this;

Weigh what convenience both of time and means

May fit us to our shape: if this should fail,

And that our drift look through our bad performance.

'Twere better not assay'd: therefore this project

Should have a back or second, that might hold

back up plan

If this did blast in proof. Soft! let me see: –

We'll make a solemn wager on your cunnings, –

Laer.'s second plan.

I ha't:

When in your motion you are hot and dry, –

As make your bouts more violent to that end, –

And that he calls for drink, I'll have prepar'd him

A chalice for the nonce; whereon but sipping,

poision his drink

If he by chance escape your venom'd stuck,

Our purpose may hold there.

Laertes plans to poison Hamlet's drink, so that when he takes a break, he'll die faster and so he can avenge his father's death!

[Enter Queen.]

How now, sweet queen!

Queen.

One woe doth tread upon another's heel,

So fast they follow: – your sister's drown'd, Laertes.

Laer.

Drown'd! O, where?

[handwritten note: Ophelia has drowned and died in the river because she couldn't mourn her father's death any longer.]

Queen.

There is a willow grows aslant a brook,

That shows his hoar leaves in the glassy stream;

There with fantastic garlands did she come

Of crowflowers, nettles, daisies, and long purples,

That liberal shepherds give a grosser name,

But our cold maids do dead men's fingers call them.

[handwritten note in left margin: where she drowned.]

There, on the pendant boughs her coronet weeds

Clamb'ring to hang, an envious sliver broke;

When down her weedy trophies and herself

Fell in the weeping brook. Her clothes spread wide;

And, mermaid-like, awhile they bore her up;

Which time she chaunted snatches of old tunes;

[handwritten note: what???]

As one incapable of her own distress,

Or like a creature native and indu'd

[handwritten note: as she was drowning she was singing, so did she commit suicide? she was singing a song to kill herself??]

Unto that element: but long it could not be

Till that her garments, heavy with their drink,

Pull'd the poor wretch from her melodious lay

To muddy death.

drowned because her clothes got very heavy

Effect: Her clothes were heavy and she drowned.

Laer.

Alas, then she is drown'd?

Queen.

Drown'd, drown'd.

Laer.

Too much of water hast thou, poor Ophelia,

And therefore I forbid my tears: but yet

It is our trick; nature her custom holds,

Let shame say what it will: when these are gone

The woman will be out. – Adieu, my lord:

I have a speech of fire, that fain would blaze,

But that this folly douts it.

Laertes mourns over Ophelia's death. He does not cry, although he's sad.

Laertes feels sad + avengeful?

[Exit.]

King.

Let's follow, Gertrude;

How much I had to do to calm his rage!

Now fear I this will give it start again;

Therefore let's follow.

doesn't really care about ophelia, just about if ~~Laer~~ Laertes is calm and ready for Hamlet

[Exeunt.]

Claudius does not care about Ophelia but he cares about the fact whether ~~the~~ he is ready to fight Hamlet or not!!

Did Ophelia die on purpose? Did she drown because of ~~the~~ her grieving over Polonius's death?

There is no right answer shakespeare leaves it this way!

ACT V.

[handwritten: at a graveyard.]

Scene I. A churchyard. *[handwritten arrow]*

[handwritten: Three sections:]
[handwritten: ① graveyard]
[handwritten: ② Hamlet's pondering life]
[handwritten: ③ Ophelia's funeral.]

[handwritten: go and get liquor later on.]

[Enter two Clowns, with spades, &c.]

1 Clown. *[handwritten: 1st gravedigger]*

[handwritten: Ophelia]

Is she to be buried in Christian burial when she wilfully

seeks her own salvation? *[handwritten: Ophelia is to have a proper burial.]*

2 Clown. *[handwritten: 2nd gravedigger]*

I tell thee she is; and therefore make her grave straight: the

crowner hath sat on her, and finds it Christian burial.

[handwritten: The graveyard is a symbol of death.]

[handwritten: talks about Ophelia]

1 Clown.

How can that be, unless she drowned herself in her own defence?

[handwritten: Ophelia has a proper burial?]

2 Clown.

Why, 'tis found so.

1 Clown.

It must be se offendendo; it cannot be else. For here lies

the point: if I drown myself wittingly, it argues an act: and an

act hath three branches; it is to act, to do, and to perform:

argal, she drowned herself wittingly.

[handwritten: Ophelia has drowned herself but why?]

[handwritten margin note: reason why Ophelia drowned.]

2 Clown.

Nay, but hear you, goodman delver, –

1 Clown.

Give me leave. Here lies the water; good: here stands the

man; good: if the man go to this water and drown himself, it is,

will he, nill he, he goes, – mark you that: but if the water come

to him and drown him, he drowns not himself; argal, he that is

not guilty of his own death shortens not his own life.

2 Clown.

But is this law?

1 Clown.

Ay, marry, is't – crowner's quest law.

2 Clown.

Will you ha' the truth on't? If this had not been a

gentlewoman, she should have been buried out o' Christian burial.

1 Clown.

Why, there thou say'st: and the more pity that great folk

should have countenance in this world to drown or hang themselves

more than their even Christian. – Come, my spade. There is no

ancient gentlemen but gardeners, ditchers, and grave-makers: they

hold up Adam's profession. *digging her grave.*

2 Clown.

Was he a gentleman?

1 Clown.

He was the first that ever bore arms.

2 Clown.

Why, he had none.

1 Clown.

What, art a heathen? How dost thou understand the Scripture?

The Scripture says Adam digg'd: could he dig without arms? I'll

put another question to thee: if thou answerest me not to the

purpose, confess thyself, –

2 Clown.

Go to.

1 Clown.

What is he that builds stronger than either the mason, the

shipwright, or the carpenter?

2 Clown.

The gallows-maker; for that frame outlives a thousand tenants.

1 Clown.

I like thy wit well, in good faith: the gallows does well;

but how does it well? it does well to those that do ill: now,

thou dost ill to say the gallows is built stronger than the

church; argal, the gallows may do well to thee. To't again, come.

2 Clown.

Who builds stronger than a mason, a shipwright, or a carpenter?

1 Clown.

Ay, tell me that, and unyoke.

2 Clown.

Marry, now I can tell.

1 Clown.

To't.

2 Clown.

Mass, I cannot tell.

[Enter Hamlet and Horatio, at a distance.]

1 Clown.

To beat

Cudgel thy brains no more about it, for your dull ass will

not mend his pace with beating; and when you are asked this

question next, say 'a grave-maker;' the houses he makes last till doomsday. Go, get thee to Yaughan; fetch me a stoup of

liquor.

[Exit Second Clown.] *goes to get a liquor.*

[Digs and sings.]

the diggers are deciding whether she needs a Christian burial. Acc

In youth when I did love, did love,

   Methought it was very sweet;

To contract, O, the time for, ah, my behove,

   O, methought there was nothing meet.

Ham.

Has this fellow no feeling of his business, that he sings at

grave-making? *← Hamlet does not know that Ophelia has died.*

Hor.

Custom hath made it in him a property of easiness.

Ham.

'Tis e'en so: the hand of little employment hath the daintier sense.

1 Clown.

[Sings.]

But age, with his stealing steps,

Hath claw'd me in his clutch,

And hath shipp'd me into the land,

As if I had never been such.

[Throws up a skull.] ← *He looks at the skull and realizes it is one of his friends?*

Ham.

That skull had a tongue in it, and could sing once: how the knave jowls it to the ground,as if 'twere Cain's jawbone, that did the first murder! This might be the pate of a politician, which this ass now o'erreaches; one that would circumvent God, might it not? ←

Hor.

It might, my lord.

Ham.

Or of a courtier, which could say 'Good morrow, sweet lord!

How dost thou, good lord?' This might be my lord such-a-one, that

praised my lord such-a-one's horse when he meant to beg

it, – might it not?

Hor.

Ay, my lord.

Ham.

Why, e'en so: and now my Lady Worm's; chapless, and knocked

about the mazard with a sexton's spade: here's fine revolution,

an we had the trick to see't. Did these bones cost no more the

breeding but to play at loggets with 'em? mine ache to think

on't.

1 Clown.

[Sings.]

A pickaxe and a spade, a spade,

For and a shrouding sheet;

O, a pit of clay for to be made

For such a guest is meet.

[Throws up another skull].

Ham.

There's another: why may not that be the skull of a lawyer? ← _talking about Yorick's skull._

Where be his quiddits now, his quillets, his cases, his tenures,

and his tricks? why does he suffer this rude knave now to knock

him about the sconce with a dirty shovel, and will not tell him

of his action of battery? Hum! This fellow might be in's time a

great buyer of land, with his statutes, his recognizances, his _Yorick's skull_

fines, his double vouchers, his recoveries: is this the fine of

his fines, and the recovery of his recoveries, to have his fine

pate full of fine dirt? will his vouchers vouch him no more of

his purchases, and double ones too, than the length and breadth

of a pair of indentures? The very conveyances of his lands will

scarcely lie in this box; and must the inheritor himself have no

more, ha?

Hor.

Not a jot more, my lord.

Ham.

Is not parchment made of sheep-skins?

Hor.

Ay, my lord, And of calf-skins too.

Ham.

They are sheep and calves which seek out assurance in that. I will speak to this fellow. – Whose grave's this, sir?

1 Clown.

Mine, sir.

[Sings.]

  O, a pit of clay for to be made

    For such a guest is meet.

Ham.

I think it be thine indeed, for thou liest in't.

1 Clown.

You lie out on't, sir, and therefore 'tis not yours: for my part,

I do not lie in't, yet it is mine.

Ham.

Thou dost lie in't, to be in't and say it is thine: 'tis for

the dead, not for the quick; therefore thou liest. ← Hamlet discovers he's lying

1 Clown.

'Tis a quick lie, sir; 't will away again from me to you.

Ham.

What man dost thou dig it for?

1 Clown.

For no man, sir.

Ham.

What woman then?

1 Clown.

For none neither.

Ham.

Who is to be buried in't?

1 Clown.

Ophelia

One that was a woman, sir; but, rest her soul, she's dead.

Ham.

How absolute the knave is! We must speak by the card, or

equivocation will undo us. By the Lord, Horatio, these three

years I have taken note of it, the age is grown so picked that

the toe of the peasant comes so near the heel of the courtier he

galls his kibe. – How long hast thou been a grave-maker?

1 Clown.

Of all the days i' the year, I came to't that day that our

last King Hamlet overcame Fortinbras.

Ham.

How long is that since?

1 Clown. ← *has no idea who Hamlet is*

Cannot you tell that? every fool can tell that: it was the

very day that young Hamlet was born, – he that is mad, and sent

into England. ← *talking about Hamlet himself*

Ham.

Ay, marry, why was be sent into England?

1 Clown.

Why, because he was mad: he shall recover his wits there;

or, if he do not, it's no great matter there.

Ham.

Why?

Clowns are crazy.

1 Clown.

'Twill not he seen in him there; there the men are as mad as he. ←

Ham.

How came he mad?

1 Clown.

Very strangely, they say.

Ham.

How strangely?

1 Clown.

Faith, e'en with losing his wits.

Ham.

Upon what ground?

1 Clown.

Why, here in Denmark: I have been sexton here, man and boy,

thirty years.

Ham.

How long will a man lie i' the earth ere he rot?

1 Clown.

Faith, if he be not rotten before he die, – as we have many

pocky corses now-a-days that will scarce hold the laying in, – he

will last you some eight year or nine year: a tanner will last

you nine year.

Ham.

Why he more than another?

1 Clown.

Why, sir, his hide is so tann'd with his trade that he will

keep out water a great while; and your water is a sore decayer of

your whoreson dead body. Here's a skull now; this skull hath lain

in the earth three-and-twenty years. ← Yorick

Ham.

Whose was it?

1 Clown.

A whoreson, mad fellow's it was: whose do you think it was?

Ham.

Nay, I know not.

1 Clown.

A pestilence on him for a mad rogue! 'a pour'd a flagon of

Rhenish on my head once. This same skull, sir, was Yorick's

skull, the king's jester. ← *Yorick has died.*

Ham.

This?

1 Clown.

E'en that.

Ham. *Yorick has died. Yorike ←*

Let me see. [Takes the skull.] Alas, poor Yorick! – I knew him,

Horatio; a fellow of infinite jest, of most excellent fancy: he

hath borne me on his back a thousand times; and now, how *abhorred*

in my imagination it is! my gorge rises at it. Here hung those

lips that I have kiss'd I know not how oft. Where be your gibes

now? your gambols? your songs? your flashes of merriment, that

were wont to set the table on a roar? Not one now, to mock your own grinning? quite chap-fallen? Now, get you to my lady's chamber, and tell her, let her paint an inch thick, to this favour she must come; make her laugh at that. – Pr'ythee, Horatio, tell me one thing.

Hor.

What's that, my lord?

Ham.

Dost thou think Alexander looked o' this fashion i' the earth?

Hor.

E'en so.

Ham.

And smelt so? Pah!

[Throws down the skull.]

Hor.

E'en so, my lord.

Ham.

To what base uses we may return, Horatio! Why may not imagination trace the noble dust of Alexander till he find it stopping a bung-hole?

Hor.

'Twere to consider too curiously to consider so.

Ham.

No, faith, not a jot; but to follow him thither with modesty enough, and likelihood to lead it: as thus: Alexander died, Alexander was buried, Alexander returneth into dust; the dust is earth; of earth we make loam; and why of that loam whereto he was converted might they not stop a beer-barrel?

Imperious Caesar, dead and turn'd to clay,

Might stop a hole to keep the wind away.

O, that that earth which kept the world in awe

Should patch a wall to expel the winter's flaw!

But soft! but soft! aside! – Here comes the king.

[Enter priests, &c, in procession; the corpse of Ophelia,

Laertes, and Mourners following; King, Queen, their Trains, &c.]

The queen, the courtiers: who is that they follow?

And with such maimed rites? This doth betoken

The corse they follow did with desperate hand

Fordo it own life: 'twas of some estate.

Couch we awhile and mark.

Ophelia's family

[Retiring with Horatio.]

Laer.

What ceremony else?

Ham.

That is Laertes,

A very noble youth: mark.

Laer.

What ceremony else?

1 Priest.

Her obsequies have been as far enlarg'd

As we have warranties: her death was doubtful;

And, but that great command o'ersways the order,

She should in ground unsanctified have lodg'd

Till the last trumpet; for charitable prayers,

Shards, flints, and pebbles should be thrown on her,

Yet here she is allowed her virgin rites, → *to be buried in sacred ground*

Her maiden strewments, and the bringing home

Of bell and burial.   *Hamlet*

[margin: doesn't read her all the rites because she might of killed herself her death was doubtful and he does]

[margin: to be buried in sacred ground]

Laer.

Must there no more be done?

1 Priest.

No more be done;

We should profane the service of the dead

To sing a requiem and such rest to her ← *he is leading the percession!*

As to peace-parted souls.

Laer.

Lay her i' the earth; –

And from her fair and unpolluted flesh

May violets spring! – I tell thee, churlish priest,

A ministering angel shall my sister be

When thou liest howling.

Ham.

What, the fair Ophelia? ← Hamlet has just realized that ophelia has died.

Queen. ← Gertrude

Sweets to the sweet: farewell.

[Scattering flowers.]

I hop'd thou shouldst have been my Hamlet's wife;

I thought thy bride-bed to have deck'd, sweet maid,

And not have strew'd thy grave.

Laer.

O, treble woe

Fall ten times treble on that cursed head

Whose wicked deed thy most ingenious sense

Depriv'd thee of! – Hold off the earth awhile,

Till I have caught her once more in mine arms:

[Leaps into the grave.]

Now pile your dust upon the quick and dead,

Till of this flat a mountain you have made,

To o'ertop old Pelion or the skyish head

Of blue Olympus.

Ham.

[Advancing.]

What is he whose grief

Bears such an emphasis? whose phrase of sorrow

Conjures the wandering stars, and makes them stand

Like wonder-wounded hearers? this is I,

Hamlet the Dane. ⟵ Hamlet

[Leaps into the grave.]

Laer.

The devil take thy soul!

[Grappling with him.]

Ham.

Thou pray'st not well.

I pr'ythee, take thy fingers from my throat;

For, though I am not splenetive and rash,

Yet have I in me something dangerous,

Which let thy wiseness fear: away thy hand!

King.

Pluck them asunder.

Queen.

Hamlet! Hamlet!

All.

Gentlemen! –

Hor.

Good my lord, be quiet.

[The Attendants part them, and they come out of the grave.]

Ham.

Why, I will fight with him upon this theme

Until my eyelids will no longer wag.

Queen.

O my son, what theme?

Ham. *He says that he*

I lov'd Ophelia; forty thousand brothers *loved*

her

Could not, with all their quantity of love, *more*

Make up my sum. – What wilt thou do for her? *than*

anyone

Hamlet really did love

Ophelia. *else did.*

King.

O, he is mad, Laertes.

Queen.

For love of God, forbear him!

Ham.

'Swounds, show me what thou'lt do:

Woul't weep? woul't fight? woul't fast? woul't tear thyself?

Woul't drink up eisel? eat a crocodile?

I'll do't. – Dost thou come here to whine?

To outface me with leaping in her grave?

Be buried quick with her, and so will I:

And, if thou prate of mountains, let them throw

Millions of acres on us, till our ground,

Singeing his pate against the burning zone,

Make Ossa like a wart! Nay, an thou'lt mouth,

I'll rant as well as thou.

Queen.

This is mere madness:

And thus a while the fit will work on him;

Anon, as patient as the female dove,

When that her golden couplets are disclos'd,

His silence will sit drooping.

Ham.

Hear you, sir;

What is the reason that you use me thus?

I lov'd you ever: but it is no matter;

Let Hercules himself do what he may,

when emotional talks smarter

emotions are smarter he turns into the scholarly Hamlet

The cat will mew, and dog will have his day.

[Exit.]

Ophelia is buried because her father wanted her to be.

King.

I pray thee, good Horatio, wait upon him. –

[Exit Horatio.]

[To Laertes] ←

is mad that Hamlet is there.

Strengthen your patience in our last night's speech;

We'll put the matter to the present push. –

Good Gertrude, set some watch over your son. –

This grave shall have a living monument:

An hour of quiet shortly shall we see;

Till then in patience our proceeding be.

Now Laertes has the perfect reason why to duel Hamlet.

[Exeunt.]

Scene II. A hall in the Castle.

[Enter Hamlet and Horatio.]

begins w/ acct. of sea voyage. Purpose? shows Hamlet's
· energy
· ability
· wit
· (new) tragic indifference for life.

Ham.

So much for this, sir: now let me see the other;

You do remember all the circumstance?

Hor.

Remember it, my lord!

Ham.

Sir, in my heart there was a kind of fighting

That would not let me sleep: methought I lay

Worse than the mutinies in the bilboes. Rashly,

something worse than any other image.

And prais'd be rashness for it, — let us know,

Our indiscretion sometime serves us well,

When our deep plots do fail; and that should teach us

There's a divinity that shapes our ends,

Rough-hew them how we will.

Hor.

That is most certain.

Ham.

Up from my cabin,

My sea-gown scarf'd about me, in the dark

Grop'd I to find out them: had my desire;

Finger'd their packet; and, in fine, withdrew

The letter he found in his pocket.

To mine own room again: making so bold,

My fears forgetting manners, to unseal

Their grand commission; where I found, Horatio,

O royal knavery! an exact command, –

Larded with many several sorts of reasons,

Importing Denmark's health, and England's too,

With, ho! such bugs and goblins in my life, –

That, on the supervise, no leisure bated,

No, not to stay the grinding of the axe,

My head should be struck off. *he thinks that he deserves to die.*

Hor.

Is't possible?

Ham.

Here's the commission: read it at more leisure.

But wilt thou bear me how I did proceed?

Hor.

I beseech you.

Ham.

Being thus benetted round with villanies, –

Or I could make a prologue to my brains,

They had begun the play, – I sat me down;

Devis'd a new commission; wrote it fair:

I once did hold it, as our statists do,

A baseness to write fair, and labour'd much

How to forget that learning; but, sir, now

It did me yeoman's service. Wilt thou know

The effect of what I wrote?

Hamlet rereads the letter that he found in his pocket.

He wrote a new letter saying that R+G should die.

Hor.

Ay, good my lord.

Ham.

An earnest conjuration from the king, –

As England was his faithful tributary;

As love between them like the palm might flourish;

As peace should still her wheaten garland wear

And stand a comma 'tween their amities;

And many such-like as's of great charge, –

That, on the view and know of these contents,

Without debatement further, more or less,

He should the bearers put to sudden death,

Not shriving-time allow'd.

He's planning to have R+G sentenced to death.

Hor.

How was this seal'd?

Ham.

Why, even in that was heaven ordinant.

I had my father's signet in my purse,

Which was the model of that Danish seal:

Folded the writ up in the form of the other;

Subscrib'd it: gave't the impression; plac'd it safely,

The changeling never known. Now, the next day

Was our sea-fight; and what to this was sequent

Thou know'st already.

Hor.

So Guildenstern and Rosencrantz go to't.

Ham.

Why, man, they did make love to this employment;

They are not near my conscience; their defeat

Does by their own insinuation grow:

'Tis dangerous when the baser nature comes

Between the pass and fell incensed points

Of mighty opposites.

Hamlet is saying that R + G basically asked for it. He makes it perfect by putting a Danish seal and his new letter looks a lot like the old one.

Hor.

Why, what a king is this!

This is the moment where Horatio knows the whole story.

Ham.

Does it not, thinks't thee, stand me now upon, —

He that hath kill'd my king, and whor'd my mother;

Popp'd in between the election and my hopes;

Thrown out his angle for my proper life,

And with such cozenage – is't not perfect conscience

To quit him with this arm? and is't not to be damn'd

To let this canker of our nature come

In further evil?

Hor.

It must be shortly known to him from England

What is the issue of the business there.

Ham.

It will be short: the interim is mine;

And a man's life is no more than to say One.

But I am very sorry, good Horatio,

That to Laertes I forgot myself;

For by the image of my cause I see

The portraiture of his: I'll court his favours:

But, sure, the bravery of his grief did put me

Into a towering passion.

Hor.

Peace; who comes here?

[Enter Osric.]

Osr. ~~Messenger~~ ← *messenger*

Your lordship is right welcome back to Denmark. ← *embodiment of stupid*

Ham.

I humbly thank you, sir. Dost know this water-fly? ← *Hamlet makes fun of Osric.*

Hor.

No, my good lord.

Ham.

Thy state is the more gracious; for 'tis a vice to know him. He hath much land, and fertile: let a beast be lord of beasts, and his crib shall stand at the king's mess; 'tis a chough; but, as I say, spacious in the possession of dirt. ← *Hamlet*

Osr.

Sweet lord, if your lordship were at leisure, I should impart a thing to you from his majesty.

Ham.

I will receive it with all diligence of spirit. Put your bonnet to his right use; 'tis for the head.

Osr.

I thank your lordship, t'is very hot.

Osric tells Hamlet about the duel.

Ham.

No, believe me, 'tis very cold; the wind is northerly.

Osr.

It is indifferent cold, my lord, indeed.

Ham.

Methinks it is very sultry and hot for my complexion.

Osr.

Exceedingly, my lord; it is very sultry, – as 'twere – I cannot

tell how. But, my lord, his majesty bade me signify to you that

he has laid a great wager on your head. Sir, this is the

matter, –

Ham.

I beseech you, remember, –

[Hamlet moves him to put on his hat.]

Osr.

Nay, in good faith; for mine ease, in good faith. Sir, here

is newly come to court Laertes; believe me, an absolute

gentleman, full of most excellent differences, of very soft

society and great showing: indeed, to speak feelingly of him, he

is the card or calendar of gentry; for you shall find in him the

continent of what part a gentleman would see.

Osric
exaggerates
about

Ham.

Sir, his definement suffers no perdition in you; – though, I

know, to divide him inventorially would dizzy the arithmetic of

memory, and yet but yaw neither, in respect of his quick sail.

But, in the verity of extolment, I take him to be a soul of great article, and his infusion of such dearth and rareness as, to make true diction of him, his semblable is his mirror, and who else would trace him, his umbrage, nothing more.

Osr.

Your lordship speaks most infallibly of him.

Ham.

The concernancy, sir? why do we wrap the gentleman in our more rawer breath?

Osr.

Sir?

Hor.

Is't not possible to understand in another tongue? You will do't, sir, really.

Ham.

What imports the nomination of this gentleman?

Osr.

Of Laertes?

Hor.

His purse is empty already; all's golden words are spent.

Ham.

Of him, sir.

Osr.

I know, you are not ignorant, –

Ham.

I would you did, sir; yet, in faith, if you did, it would not much approve me. – Well, sir.

Osr.

You are not ignorant of what excellence Laertes is, –

Ham.

I dare not confess that, lest I should compare with him in excellence; but to know a man well were to know himself.

Osr.

I mean, sir, for his weapon; but in the imputation laid on him by them, in his meed he's unfellowed. ← *Osric is impressed by Laertes*

Ham.

What's his weapon?

Osr.

→ *fencing sword*
Rapier and dagger. ← *Laertes is good at*

Ham.

That's two of his weapons: – but well.

Osr.

The challenge
The king, sir, hath wager'd with him six Barbary horses: against the which he has imponed, as I take it, six French rapiers and poniards, with their assigns, as girdle, hangers, and so: three of the carriages, in faith, are very dear to fancy,

very responsive to the hilts, most delicate carriages, and of

very liberal conceit.

Ham.

What call you the carriages?

Hor.

I knew you must be edified by the margent ere you had done.

Osr.

The carriages, sir, are the hangers.

Ham.

The phrase would be more german to the matter if we could

carry cannon by our sides. I would it might be hangers till then.

But, on: six Barbary horses against six French swords, their

assigns, and three liberal conceited carriages: that's the French

bet against the Danish: why is this all imponed, as you call it?

Challenge

Osr.

The king, sir, hath laid that, in a dozen passes between

your and him, he shall not exceed you three hits: he hath

laid on twelve for nine; and it would come to immediate trial

if your lordship would vouchsafe the answer.

Ham.

How if I answer no? ← *what if I say no?*

Osr.

I mean, my lord, the opposition of your person in trial.

Ham.

Sir, I will walk here in the hall: if it please his majesty,

it is the breathing time of day with me: let the foils be

brought, the gentleman willing, and the king hold his purpose, *king Hamlet.*

I will win for him if I can; if not, I will gain nothing but my

shame and the odd hits. ← *Hamlet fights for king Hamlet*

Osr.

Shall I re-deliver you e'en so?

Ham.

To this effect, sir; after what flourish your nature will.

Osr.

I commend my duty to your lordship.

Ham.

Yours, yours.

[Exit Osric.]

He does well to commend it himself; there are no tongues else

for's turn.

Hor.

This lapwing runs away with the shell on his head.

Ham.

He did comply with his dug before he suck'd it. Thus has he, – and

many more of the same bevy that I know the drossy age dotes on, –

only got the tune of the time and outward habit of encounter;

a kind of yesty collection, which carries them through and

through the most fanned and winnowed opinions; and do but blow

them to their trial, the bubbles are out,

[Enter a Lord.]

Lord.

My lord, his majesty commended him to you by young Osric,

who brings back to him that you attend him in the hall: he sends

to know if your pleasure hold to play with Laertes, or that you

will take longer time.

The Lord asks Hamlet if he's ready to fight Laertes or not?

Ham.

I am constant to my purposes; they follow the king's pleasure:

Hamlet's father

if his fitness speaks, mine is ready; now or whensoever, provided

I be so able as now.

Lord.

The King and Queen and all are coming down.

Ham.

In happy time.

Lord.

The queen desires you to use some gentle entertainment to

Laertes before you fall to play.

Ham.

She well instructs me.

[Exit Lord.]

Hor.

You will lose this wager, my lord. ← *Horatio thinks that Hamlet won't win the match.*

Ham.

I do not think so; since he went into France I have been in

continual practice: I shall win at the odds. But thou wouldst not

think how ill all's here about my heart: but it is no matter.

foreshadowing   *fore-shadowing his fate.*

Hor.

Nay, good my lord, –

Ham.

It is but foolery; but it is such a kind of gain-giving as would perhaps trouble a woman.

Hor.

If your mind dislike anything, obey it: I will forestall their repair hither, and say you are not fit.

Ham.

Not a whit, we defy augury: there's a special providence in the fall of a sparrow. If it be now, 'tis not to come; if it be not to come, it will be now; if it be not now, yet it will come: the readiness is all: since no man has aught of what he leaves, what is't to leave betimes?

claud. Gier.
↑ ↑

[Enter King, Queen, Laertes, Lords, Osric, and Attendants with foils &c.]

King. ←— The king is still making a show.

Come, Hamlet, come, and take this hand from me.

[The King puts Laertes' hand into Hamlet's.]

Ham.

Give me your pardon, sir: I have done you wrong:

But pardon't, as you are a gentleman.

This presence knows, and you must needs have heard,

How I am punish'd with sore distraction.

What I have done

That might your nature, honour, and exception

Roughly awake, I here proclaim was madness.

Was't Hamlet wrong'd Laertes? Never Hamlet:

If Hamlet from himself be ta'en away,

And when he's not himself does wrong Laertes,

Then Hamlet does it not, Hamlet denies it.

Who does it, then? His madness: if't be so,

Hamlet is of the faction that is wrong'd;

His madness is poor Hamlet's enemy.

Sir, in this audience,

Let my disclaiming from a purpos'd evil

Free me so far in your most generous thoughts

That I have shot my arrow o'er the house

Hamlet begs for his (Laertes's) forgiveness

And hurt my brother.

Laer.

I am satisfied in nature,

Whose motive, in this case, should stir me most

To my revenge. But in my terms of honour

I stand aloof; and will no reconcilement

Till by some elder masters of known honour

I have a voice and precedent of peace

To keep my name ungor'd. But till that time

I do receive your offer'd love like love,

And will not wrong it.

Ham.

I embrace it freely;

And will this brother's wager frankly play. —

Give us the foils; come on.

Laer.

Come, one for me.

[handwritten margin notes: Laertes accepts Hamlet's apology. what's at stake: the game is still on.]

Ham.

I'll be your foil, Laertes; in mine ignorance

Your skill shall, like a star in the darkest night,

Stick fiery off indeed.

Laer.

You mock me, sir.

Ham.

No, by this hand.

King.

Give them the foils, young Osric. Cousin Hamlet,

You know the wager?   *He switches the swords.*

Ham.

Very well, my lord;

Your grace has laid the odds o' the weaker side.

King.

I do not fear it; I have seen you both;

But since he's better'd, we have therefore odds.

Laer.

This is too heavy, let me see another.

Ham.

This likes me well. These foils have all a length?

[They prepare to play.]

Osr.

Ay, my good lord.

King.

Set me the stoups of wine upon that table, –

If Hamlet give the first or second hit,

Or quit in answer of the third exchange,

Let all the battlements their ordnance fire;

The king shall drink to Hamlet's better breath;

And in the cup an union shall he throw,

Richer than that which four successive kings

In Denmark's crown have worn. Give me the cups;

And let the kettle to the trumpet speak,

The trumpet to the cannoneer without,

The cannons to the heavens, the heavens to earth,

'Now the king drinks to Hamlet.' – Come, begin: –

And you, the judges, bear a wary eye.

Ham.

Come on, sir.

Laer.

Come, my lord.

[They play.] ← The duel begins

Ham.

One.

Laer.

No.

Ham.

Judgment!

Osr.

A hit, a very palpable hit. *[handwritten: sensible]*

Laer.

Well; – again.

King.

Stay, give me drink. – Hamlet, this pearl is thine; *[handwritten: cup of poison.]*

Here's to thy health. – *[handwritten: Claudius poisons the cup and tries to persuade him to drink it.]*

[Trumpets sound, and cannon shot off within.]

Give him the cup.

Ham.

I'll play this bout first; set it by awhile. –

Come. – Another hit; what say you? *[handwritten: HAM. is not quite ready to drink]*

[They play.]

Laer.

A touch, a touch, I do confess.

King.

Our son shall win.

Queen.

He's fat, and scant of breath. —

Here, Hamlet, take my napkin, rub thy brows:

The queen carouses to thy fortune, Hamlet.

Ham.

Good madam!

King.

Gertrude, do not drink. ← _Gertrude drinks the wine and falls dead to the ground._

Queen.

I will, my lord; I pray you pardon me.

317 | P a g e

King.

[Aside.] It is the poison'd cup; it is too late.

Gertrude drank the poisoned cup.

Ham.

I dare not drink yet, madam; by-and-by.

Queen.

Come, let me wipe thy face.

Laer.

My lord, I'll hit him now.

King.

I do not think't.

Laer.

[Aside.] And yet 'tis almost 'gainst my conscience. ← *there is a glimmer of hope.*

Ham.

Come, for the third, Laertes: you but dally; ← *mess around.*

I pray you pass with your best violence:

I am afeard you make a wanton of me.

Laer.

Say you so? come on.

[They play.]

Osr.

Nothing, neither way.

Laer.

Have at you now!

[Laertes wounds Hamlet; then, in scuffling, they

change rapiers, and Hamlet wounds Laertes.]

Laertes stabbed Hamlet. Hamlet takes Laertes's sword and hits him.

King.

Part them; they are incens'd.

Ham.

Nay, come again!

[The Queen falls.] ← *Gertrude dies.*

Osr.

Look to the queen there, ho!

Hor.

They bleed on both sides. – How is it, my lord?

Osr.

How is't, Laertes?

Laer.

Why, as a woodcock to my own springe, Osric;

I am justly kill'd with mine own treachery.

Ham.

How does the Queen?

King.

She swoons to see them bleed.

Claudius still puts on a show.

Queen.

No, no! the drink, the drink! – O my dear Hamlet! –

The drink, the drink! – I am poison'd.

← *Gertrude drinks the wine and dies.*

↑ *everyone hears her.*

[Dies.]

Ham.

O villany! – Ho! let the door be lock'd:

Treachery! seek it out.

[Laertes falls.] ← *Laertes's concious gets the better of him.*

Laer.

It is here, Hamlet: Hamlet, thou art slain;

Hint. Laertes dies

No medicine in the world can do thee good;

In thee there is not half an hour of life;

The treacherous instrument is in thy hand,

Unbated and envenom'd: the foul practice

Hath turn'd itself on me; lo, here I lie,

Never to rise again: thy mother's poison'd:

I can no more: – the king, the king's to blame.

Ham.

The point envenom'd too! –

Then, venom, to thy work. ←—

[Stabs the King.] ←— *Hamlet kills Claudius, with the poisoned sword.*

Osric and Lords.

Treason! treason!

King.

O, yet defend me, friends! I am but hurt. ←— *Hamlet stabs Claudius.*

Ham.

Here, thou incestuous, murderous, damned Dane,

Drink off this potion. – Is thy union here?

Follow my mother.

[King dies.]

Laer.

He is justly serv'd;

It is a poison temper'd by himself. –

Exchange forgiveness with me, noble Hamlet:

Mine and my father's death come not upon thee,

Nor thine on me!

Laertes asks for Hamlet's forgiveness, and Ham. accepts it.

[Dies.]

Ham.

Heaven make thee free of it! I follow thee. –

I am dead, Horatio. – Wretched queen, adieu! –

You that look pale and tremble at this chance,

That are but mutes or audience to this act,

Had I but time, – as this fell sergeant, death,

Is strict in his arrest, – O, I could tell you, –

But let it be. – Horatio, I am dead;

Thou liv'st; report me and my cause aright

To the unsatisfied.

Hamlet is saying his last words.

Hor. ← *is the one who lives on, and knows everything.*

Never believe it:

I am more an antique Roman than a Dane. –

Here's yet some liquor left.

Ham.

As thou'rt a man,

Give me the cup; let go; by heaven, I'll have't. –

O good Horatio, what a wounded name,

Things standing thus unknown, shall live behind me!

If thou didst ever hold me in thy heart,

Absent thee from felicity awhile,

And in this harsh world draw thy breath in pain,

To tell my story. – ←

Hamlet asks Horatio to tell his story, and dies.

[March afar off, and shot within.]

What warlike noise is this?

Osr.

coming from Poland.

Young Fortinbras, with conquest come from Poland,

To the ambassadors of England gives

This warlike volley.

Ham.

O, I die, Horatio;

The potent poison quite o'er-crows my spirit:

I cannot live to hear the news from England;

But I do prophesy the election lights

On Fortinbras: he has my dying voice;

So tell him, with the occurrents, more and less,

Which have solicited. – the rest is silence.

Hamlet dies, and has the right to name his successor; Fortinbras.

[Dies.]

Hor.

Now cracks a noble heart. – Good night, sweet prince,

And flights of angels sing thee to thy rest!

Why does the drum come hither?

Horatio's prayer to Hamlet.

[March within.]

[Enter Fortinbras, the English Ambassadors, and others.]

Fort.

Where is this sight?

Hor.

What is it you will see?

If aught of woe or wonder, cease your search.

Fort.

This quarry cries on havoc. – O proud death,

What feast is toward in thine eternal cell,

That thou so many princes at a shot

So bloodily hast struck?

1 Ambassador.

The sight is dismal;

And our affairs from England come too late:

The ears are senseless that should give us hearing,

To tell him his commandment is fulfill'd

That Rosencrantz and Guildenstern are dead:

Where should we have our thanks?

Hor.

Not from his mouth,

Had it the ability of life to thank you:

He never gave commandment for their death.

But since, so jump upon this bloody question,

You from the Polack wars, and you from England,

Are here arriv'd, give order that these bodies

High on a stage be placed to the view;

And let me speak to the yet unknowing world

How these things came about: so shall you hear

Of carnal, bloody and unnatural acts;

Of accidental judgments, casual slaughters;

Of deaths put on by cunning and forc'd cause;

And, in this upshot, purposes mistook

Fall'n on the inventors' heads: all this can I

Truly deliver.

Horatio has the whole story, with the details.

Fort.

Let us haste to hear it,

And call the noblest to the audience.

For me, with sorrow I embrace my fortune:

I have some rights of memory in this kingdom,

Which now, to claim my vantage doth invite me.

Hor.

Of that I shall have also cause to speak,

And from his mouth whose voice will draw on more:

But let this same be presently perform'd,

Even while men's minds are wild: lest more mischance

On plots and errors happen.

Fort.

Let four captains

Bear Hamlet like a soldier to the stage;

For he was likely, had he been put on,

To have prov'd most royally: and, for his passage,

The soldiers' music and the rites of war

Speak loudly for him. –

Take up the bodies. – Such a sight as this

Becomes the field, but here shows much amiss.

Hamlet will be buried as a soilder.

Hamlet

Go, bid the soldiers shoot. ← this is to be
an honorable right
of passage.

[A dead march.]

100?s
PART A ← Literal
PART B ← Puns

[Exeunt, bearing off the dead bodies; after the which a peal of

ordnance is shot off.]

Fortinbras takes
over the kingdom.

He is an honorable.

CPSIA information can be obtained at www.ICGtesting.com
Printed in the USA
BVOW04s1419190913

331495BV00001B/367/P